MW00575196

Mosaic

A Ministry Handbook for a Globalizing World

Jared Looney & Seth Bouchelle

Editor: Andrew Wood

Urban Ministry in the 21st Century

Volume 9

Urban Loft Publishers | Skyforest, CA

Mosaic

Mosaic
A Ministry Handbook for a Globalizing World

Urban Loft Publishers
P.O. Box 6
Skyforest, CA 92385
www.urbanloftpublishers.com

Senior Editors: Stephen Burris & Kendi Howells Douglas
Editor: Andrew Wood
Copy Editor: Kara Hardin
Graphics: Elisabeth Clevenger & Amber McKinley

ISBN-13: 978-0-9973717-5-8

Made in the U.S.

Acknowledgements

Jared:

I'm grateful for Hylma and Adalia who are an enduring support. Thank you to our co-laborers in Global City Mission Initiative who are such an important part of this story of reaching the nations in our cities. I also appreciate Impact Ministries in Houston and Manhattan Church of Christ in NYC who were formative laboratories for me in experiencing international churches in global cities, and I am so grateful for all who participated in the church planting journey of Bronx Fellowship which laid the foundation for this work today.

Seth:

Many thanks to our team in New York City for allowing us to use the many stories and case studies that arise from our shared ministry and that are used here in this book. I'm grateful for Gabe, Tyler, and others who shared their experiences in the city with me, and I deeply appreciate all of the conversation partners who have helped us form the ideas that fill the pages of this book. Thank you, Carey, for your editing and encouragement throughout this process. I couldn't have done this work otherwise.

Endorsements

American Christians woke up one day and discovered the world had come to North America bringing an almost endless variety of cultures and values. But do we have a Gospel that connects with these world citizens who are now our new neighbors? The authors answer with a resounding "Yes" and what's more, they tell us HOW. A truly visionary book!

-Randy Harris, Spiritual Director, Abilene Christian University College of Biblical Studies and Author of "Living Jesus."

Wake up! We are all cross-cultural missionaries! If we don't apply what Jared and Seth teach as we meet our Persian neighbors, hang out with our Singaporean colleagues, or have dinner with our Laotian in-laws, we will have serious problems helping them and others fall in love with Jesus as we navigate an increasingly multicultural world.

-Paul D. Watson, Co-Founder of Contagious Disciple-Making and Author

Prophetic. Pastoral. Practical. Having spent my life looking at the issues of cross-cultural work, I find in this book the vital ingredients for effective ministry: integrity; sensitivity to the underlying issues of message, creation, and culture; and profound respect for each human being. I highly recommend this volume.

-Landon Saunders, President of Heartbeat Ministries

This book is important. It's a fairly comprehensive glimpse into the cutting edge of the Mission of God. Seth and Jared are deeply theologically rooted and methodologically astute. Most importantly they are daily practitioners of making disciples of Jesus and helping create churches that are formed around the actual people who comprise the church.

Their stories are inspiring and their strategies sound a lot like the book of Acts as if it was lived out in New York City. The most important thing this book can do is help spark something that has sadly gone missing in most Western Christian ecclesiology; a Christian imagination for the world and God's people.

Seth and Jared remind us, the most exciting shapes that the church can take haven't been thought of yet.

-Jonathan Storment, Minister, Highland Church of
Christ and Author of "How to Start a Riot."

Series Preface

Urban Mission in the 21st Century is a series of monographs that addresses key issues facing those involved in urban ministry whether it be in the slums, squatter communities, *favelas*, or in immigrant neighborhoods. It is our goal to bring fresh ideas, a theological basis, and best practices in urban mission as we reflect on our changing urban world. The contributors to this series bring a wide-range of ideas, experiences, education, international perspectives, and insight into the study of the growing field of urban ministry. These contributions fall into four very general areas: 1--the biblical and theological basis for urban ministry; 2--best practices currently in use and anticipated in the future by urban scholar/activists who are living working and studying in the context of cities; 3--personal experiences and observations based on urban ministry as it is currently being practiced; and 4--a forward view toward where we are headed in the decades ahead in the expanding and developing field of urban mission. This series is intended for educators, graduate students, theologians, pastors, and serious students of urban ministry.

More than anything, these contributions are creative attempts to help Christians strategically and creatively think about how we can better reach our world that is now more urban than rural. We do not see theology and practice as separate and distinct. Rather, we see sound practice growing out of a healthy vibrant theology that seeks to understand God's world as it truly is as we move further into the twenty-first century. Contributors interact with the best scholarly literature available at the time of writing while making application to specific contexts in which they live and work.

Each book in the series is intended to be a thought-provoking work that represents the author's experience and perspective on urban ministry in a particular context. The editors have chosen those who bring this rich diversity of perspectives to this series. It is our hope and prayer that each book in this series will challenge, enrich, provoke, and cause the reader to dig deeper into subjects that bring the reader to a deeper understanding of our urban world and the ministry the church is called to perform in that new world.

Dr. Kendi Howells Douglas and Stephen Burris,
Urban Mission in the 21st Century Series Co-Editors

Table of Contents

Introduction

Several years ago I (Jared) was working in Houston, TX, and a nearby church came to our leadership to seek help. Our ministry specialized in working in the city's poorest communities. We intentionally focused on some of the toughest neighborhoods, and as a bilingual ministry, we spent a great deal of time serving people from a variety of cultures and backgrounds. The church that came to our team for assistance had been gathering as a congregation in their location for decades. The membership was aging, and the congregation was solely made up of white middle-class Americans. The community around them, however, was now predominantly composed of Spanish-speaking families who had recently immigrated from countries in Latin America. The first language of the church was English. The first language of the neighborhood was Spanish. They sang different types of songs, ate different types of food, and had vastly different cultural experiences of living in Texas. During the church's life cycle, the neighborhood had completely changed. This church still hoped to make a difference, but truthfully, they did not even know where to begin.

A few years after moving to New York City as an urban missionary, I had the opportunity to sit and visit with a leader of a large urban ministry located in the Southeastern United States. He represented a ministry that had started when Christian volunteers from the suburbs went into predominantly Black housing projects to start Bible classes with youth in the community. It had begun many years earlier as a cross-cultural effort. The ministry had grown and expanded over a couple of decades and many lives had experienced the transformational power of the Gospel of Christ. However, as this leader and I sat and talked, he shared some of the new challenges facing his congregation. He explained that they knew how to serve the struggling populations living in the housing projects of their city. They had done so successfully for years. Many had come to know Jesus as their Lord and had bowed their knees to Him in worship and in obedience. Children had been mentored. Families had been renewed. Salvation had been preached to many hundreds. It was a ministry that had thrived for years. Nevertheless, they were facing new challenges. This veteran urban ministry leader shared that the community around them had begun to change radically and was a different neighborhood than the one they had once known. Despite their history of successfully crossing one historical cultural barrier they were now faced with a number of foreign neighbors with whom they did not know how to relate. He said to me, "The community around our building has changed. Our church's neighbors are now Indians, Chinese, and Hispanics. We really do not know what to do."

From Dallas to Chicago and from Philadelphia to Sacramento, church leaders are facing the challenges of demographic shifts in North America. These are many of the same challenges that we as missionaries have been dealing with for well over a decade in New York City as common everyday encounters. We hope, here, to offer some practical help for Christian leaders who desire to reach out to their community but who were never formally trained as cross-cultural missionaries nor studied cultural anthropology. Both authors work with Global City Mission Initiative, which focuses on reaching out cross-culturally in multicultural cities. Our team works both in multiethnic communities—where we encounter any number of ethnic heritages and cultural backgrounds—and in ethnic enclaves where a specific nation, language, or region of the world is concentrated within our city. As we began telling our stories about leading Bible studies with Chinese seekers, attending festivals with Bengalis, mentoring Central Americans as new disciples, or building friendships with our West Indian neighbors, we also began hearing their stories: stories of Christian leaders hosting South Asian congregations in their church building, of encounters with West African Muslims in their grocery store or shopping mall, or of suburbs being transformed as Chinese or Latin American communities. These communities have begun to emerge as a new and exciting presence in the neighborhoods near their church building, workplace, or home.

In art, mosaics are works created by a vast collection of tiny fragments contributing different colors and textures to the whole. Similarly, our cities are cultural mosaics representing an array of subcultures that together display the image of the global city. As we encounter the diversity of the city, our evangelistic efforts equally represent a mosaic as different choices of words, styles, and expressions each pointing to the image of Christ. Christians who may have previously imagined cross-cultural ministry as something that takes place an ocean away are now encountering different cultures when they cross the street.

While there have been a myriad of great works written on cross-cultural ministry (and we stand on the shoulders of the authors of so many of these works), one of our observations during conversations with Christian leaders around the country is that there is an ongoing need for resources to help the church address the realities of cross-cultural ministry within our cities and sort through the nuances of working at the intersection of cultures in increasingly diverse diasporas. We have set out to offer a resource for ministry in a much more globalized world than the one that existed even a couple of decades ago. Many works that have provided a foundational understanding for addressing various cultures have been influential to us as we have stumbled across our neighbors originating from nearly every continent. We are building on the foundation of the missionary enterprise as the Gospel has moved across cultural barriers throughout our world. In a globalized urban context, however, the emerging reality is that there is an *intersection* as well as blending of cultures. Culture in a global age is anything but monolithic. The one constant is change. We are addressing ministry practices and an attentiveness to culture at the dynamic global intersection now playing out in local neighborhoods that is just around the corner from the average American church.

New immigrants are regularly arriving in both urban and suburban neighborhoods, and simultaneously new subcultures are frequently emerging in North American cities. Practical books and articles written to assist Christian leaders to address the growing diversity and respond as local missionaries to their neighbors from around the world are an important resource. They help the church engage its new context in local evangelism. Indeed, the majority of mission texts on reaching immigrant communities have only begun to appear on the shelves in recent years. There continues to be a need for written works to offer help to churches and Christian leaders who have the desire to live as missionaries within their neighborhoods and cities. As Christian leaders seek resources for addressing cross-cultural ministry in communities that were once homogenous neighborhoods, there is an equal need to become adaptable to cultural change at the intersection of cultures in diverse metropolitan regions.

Books on cross-cultural evangelism and church planting in North America should continue to be written, and they continue to contribute to our understanding of ministry among the nations living next door. Still, there is an ongoing need to share practical experiences and to update ministry resources to help evangelists in North American cities who are encountering a range of cultures in a context of constant change and shifting demographics. We seek to provide a resource for Christian leaders who have recognized that a cross-cultural mission fields are now present in their own backyards and who desire to grow in their ability to incarnate the Gospel among their culturally different neighbors. Our intent for this volume is to provide a practical guidebook for becoming cultural learners and for navigating the issues of cross-cultural ministry across diverse communities in North American cities.

As missionaries in New York City, our daily lives involve friendships with individuals and families who have arrived in the city from virtually every region of the planet. Living at the edge of this globalized missionary engagement, we desired to provide a text that could introduce practices for cross-cultural ministry and raise awareness of issues likely to be encountered by Christian leaders who, like us, have become cross-cultural missionaries in their own backyard. It is strikingly obvious that opportunities for cross-cultural mission are now at the doorstep of countless churches across North America. Few local ministry settings are exempt from encountering culturally different pockets of people in their city or region. The ability to go to all nations—and the responsibility that entails—is now a local reality. The image of a global society in the United States is no longer solely concentrated in New York, Chicago, or Los Angeles, but increasingly reflected in cities such as Dallas–Fort Worth, Nashville, and Columbus.

Stull & Broadway remark, "Throughout most of the twentieth century, the availability of jobs and social support networks meant that immigration was largely confined to urban areas in California, New York, Illinois, Florida, and Texas." However, since the last decade of the twentieth century, immigrants have been flooding into states not traditionally thought of as multicultural centers, such as Georgia, Tennessee, North Carolina, Nevada, and similar locations that would previously have been considered unconventional for immigrant settlements (2008, pp. 116–118). In the past, many churches might have assumed that ethnic enclaves were just a phenomenon that formed in the central city. However, a stroll through the refugee communities of Clarksville, Georgia (just outside Atlanta), lunch in Chinese suburban enclaves east of the city of Los Angeles, or a casual drive through the predominantly Korean areas of Fort Lee, New Jersey across the Hudson River from Manhattan, provide just a few examples of the rearranging of American demographics through expanding metropolitan regions. Where there were once homogenous suburbs contrasted with multiethnic inner-cities, metropolitan areas have become vast urban expanses of cultural diversity. "Many of the newest, largest destinations, such as Atlanta, Las Vegas, and Charlotte, are places with no history of or identity with immigration. Other metropolitan areas, such as Sacramento, Minneapolis-St. Paul, and Seattle, once important gateways in the early part of the

20th century, have recently re-emerged as major new destinations" (Singer, Hardwick, & Brettell, p. 1).

Many Christian leaders serving in metropolitan areas across the United States don't need us to inform them that the neighborhoods in their city are becoming increasingly international. They already know. They are experiencing a growing ethnic and cultural diversity when they drive to the grocery store, visit a museum, or pull their car into a gas station. Many churches desire to reach out with the Gospel of Christ to their nearby communities, but they are asking the question, "Where do we start?" This work addresses that very question. If we were to start again, these are the things we have seen take place in ministry that we wish we knew at the beginning. We hope that you benefit from hearing our experiences, not only as we reflect upon successes but also the inherent value of learning from failures. Indeed, if we are to cross-cultures entering into unfamiliar experiences, we must redeem and embrace a willingness to fail. These moments are some of the biggest lessons that lead to increasingly effective ministry when entering a space that is culturally different from our own. It is our hope that this book better enables you to enter into ministry across cultures—having a clearer sense of who your new neighbors are and how you might begin to share the Gospel with them.

Chapter 1

First Things

Today, cross-cultural relationships are a normal part of daily life in many American cities. We, the authors, work as missionaries for Global City Mission Initiative (GCMI), planting churches among the global diaspora in the city. We do this with the hope of seeing disciple-making movements spread among the unreached cities and people groups of the world. Because culture is a powerful force, pervading every aspect of our perception of the world, it is important for us to stay attentive to the role culture plays both in our own lives and in the lives of our friends and neighbors. We are all products of culture as well as its carriers. One way to define culture is "knowledge that is learned and shared and that people use to generate behavior and interpret experience" (McCurdy, Spradley, & Shandy, 2004, p. 5). Numerous descriptions and definitions of culture have been offered (Luzbetak, 2015, pp. 133–159). The simplest definition, though, may be that culture is the means through which we understand the experiences of our communities and navigate the changes taking place in the world. When a local church begins to engage a nearby community of new refugees or attempts to serve an ethnic enclave emerging near where their church assembles, understanding culture is an essential part of the focus involved in the ministry. Encountering culture is unavoidable as we swim within our own cultural currents.

Mosaic

Any time we reach out to someone from a different background, we are likely crossing cultures in initiating that relationship.

Culture is something that is learned. It is a heritage we absorb. Culture is a shared perspective and experience. It is lived together. Culture produces specific behaviors that reflect certain patterns and identification, and culture gives us the interpretive lens for understanding our experiences (McCurdy et al., 2004, pp. 6–7). When we represent the Gospel to a specific community of people, we are wading through the depths of culture. No one lives outside of culture; therefore, every ministry encounter includes an encounter with a person's cultural world. "Studying a culture means understanding the categories, assumptions, and logic the people use to construct their world" (Hiebert, Shaw, & Tienou, 2000, p. 22). This book is an attempt to help Christian leaders think about the various cultures they are engaging in order to form effective ministry plans in culturally diverse cities.

"Culture is the way life is organized to give meaning to a particular group of people in their environment.... Culture is a person's second nature. Sensitivity to another's culture is, then, at least a matter of respect for the person and therefore incumbent on the Christian missionary" (Roembke, 2000, pp. 13–14). As American Christians realize the emerging opportunities to love their neighbors from around the globe who reside in their local neighborhoods, gaining an understanding of missionary engagement is increasingly important. However, "cultural awareness" is not always easy since culture is internalized as patterns of thinking and behaving that are believed to be "natural"—simply the way things are" (Stewart & Bennett, 1991, p.

x). It is not uncommon for one to classify one's own view as "normal" and differing ways of seeing the world as wholly "other."

One of the significant challenges for the American church today is to adopt its inherent identity as a missionary people and learn to appreciate the mosaic of cultures and subcultures that make up our contemporary world. Many of our newest neighbors will not automatically share even some of our most basic assumptions. I (Seth) remember seeing a short-term missions group doing evangelism in a neighborhood where I commonly work. The community is approximately half Latino and half South Asian Muslim. These young people were trying to start spiritual interactions with my neighbors, but their attempts to initiate conversation almost all began by asking individuals on the street, "What are you doing to have your sins forgiven?" Those of us from a Christian background understand the intention of this question, and see where these student missionaries were headed in their Gospel presentation. Among my Muslim and (mostly secular) Latino neighbors, I remember seeing much confusion and even offense in their reactions to these attempts. They had no basic assumption that they were sinners or needed to be forgiven. Many of them did not even understand the question and were annoyed that they were being bothered by such an irrelevant inquiry. To turn the analysis around, we might say that the short-term missionaries had also failed to share a basic assumption of my neighbors: that intimate disclosure and spiritual questions are reserved for individuals who are known and trusted. It would be a rare individual among my neighbors who would reveal their own feelings of brokenness to a complete stranger.

The task of clearly communicating the Gospel becomes increasingly complex as the landscape of our own context transforms. In our present age of globalization, culture is no longer a monolithic reality dominated by a single voice, and we are increasingly residents of multicultural cities. We are immersed in a dizzying diversity of values, language, and ideas. In a globalized world, events and experiences can be understood in vastly disparate terms within the same communities. City life generates an array of subcultures, creating great potential for new cultural groups to emerge, whether through new waves of migration, cultural assimilation processes that are drawn out over generations, or cultures combining to form new hybrid subcultures.

For those living in this new metropolitan landscape, rarely does any neighborhood or any individual have the luxury of understanding life through a singular perspective. Something I (Seth) perceive as neutral or normal may feel devastating to my Muslim neighbor. For my Yemeni butcher, civil unrest in Sana'a, has names of family and friends attached to it, although it barely makes it across my Facebook feed. Since my barber is Bangladeshi, my baker is Albanian, and my favorite barista is Irish, I have learned to watch world news differently. Truly, to understand the nature of our world, it has become increasingly important for us to analyze (as well as to appreciate) culture, both our own and our neighbors'. And this is all the more imperative for the worker of the Gospel; if my neighbor and I cannot be expected to understand and respond to the nightly news with any sense of solidarity, how much more challenging will it be for us to engage the good news of God working through Jesus Christ?

This inquiry into Christ's relationship with culture is as old as Christianity itself, and we do not expect to solve that issue here. Nor do we expect this book to be a definitive anthropological work. That is not the purpose of this text. There are many great research projects about culture; this is not meant to represent an in depth academic analysis of that sort. Rather, what follows is meant as a practical field-guide for navigating the nuances of cross-cultural ministry among the diverse ethnic groups arriving in our cities. We desire to provide a resource for the growing number of Christian leaders who now realize their local ministry context has become a significantly different place and are seeking ways to navigate this new world in the neighborhood they once knew. As our planet becomes a more interconnected and mobile world and a more urban place, change is the constant we can count on. Much of this book is drawn from our experiences of working for God's kingdom among the global diasporas in New York City, while also integrating some common ethnographic practices in addition to insights from applicable studies. While we have drawn from well-known anthropological practices, the majority of this work is based on the lessons we have learned during our first-hand experiences and observations serving among diverse international populations now living and working in North American cities. One of the lessons that serving among diverse peoples in a global environment has taught us is the need for highly adaptive frameworks. Naturally, we have also included practices that are widely recognized in missionary research as essential tools for discovering inroads to culturally different communities. We also recognize in producing this book that much of the territory we are exploring together is still evolving, especially regarding cross-cultural ministry as a local experience for the

American church. Much of the literature associated with diaspora missions (i.e., mission work among immigrant populations) has only begun to emerge in recent years, and for many Christian leaders and churches in the United States, cross-cultural ministry on a day-to-day basis is a new discovery. We hope that as we share what we are experiencing and observing in conversations within the missions community, we will continue learning in fellowship with our readers. Furthermore, we have sought to anchor our discussion in principles and practical frameworks rather than prescriptive tactics since we recognize the considerable differences from city to city, neighborhood to neighborhood, and in the variety of cross-cultural experiences.

To summarize: We would like to offer some tools and templates that have helped us navigate the difficulties of cross-cultural ministry in North America and have produced good fruit in our evangelistic and disciple-making efforts. The stories and case studies that follow are adapted from our team's ministry experiences among immigrant communities and ethnic networks in the city and are in no way exhaustive or definitive in their claims about any particular culture. Before we move forward, however, it may be helpful to define some of the terms and concepts used in the remainder of the book.

Culture as Myth

For some years I (Seth) had the following plaque on my office wall:
"Two Myths about September 11th":
1. There is a nation which has stood for generations as the protector of truth and freedom in the world. Because of envy and hatred, an insidious cult planned and carried out an attack against these heroes, in an attempt to destroy them. Although

many lives were lost, these defenders of justice survived, and now they seek to destroy this evil and put an end to oppression wherever it is found.

2. The world is overrun by an evil empire [that] seeks to exploit and to dominate all who do not bow to its culture and laws. A collection of rebels who are still faithful to God banded together to unmask the power of the empire and gave their lives to demonstrate to the world that the empire could be overcome. Now these defenders of justice carry on in the name of their fallen heroes, seeking to destroy this evil and put an end to the oppression of the empire wherever it is found."

I (Jared) remember September 11, 2001 very well. I had only moved to New York City two and a half months earlier. In the days that followed 9/11, a sadness fell over the city, and 8 million people shared a collective experience of mourning and grief. To this very day I can recall the rush of feelings I had, and I doubt I will ever truly forget the surge of emotions that followed after that Tuesday morning. My wife watched the second plane fly into the building from her office window in Midtown Manhattan, and I recall with intense clarity watching U.S. fighter jets patrolling the skies above my neighborhood. It is difficult to speak of 9/11 without emotion and without recalling every sensation that came and went during that period. Yet, as we take a step back and think about culture, it is obvious that different people from different cultures and societies may actually interpret these events quite differently.

Regardless of where you come from, hopefully it is apparent that neither of the narratives above is an unbiased interpretation of the events in question. Both are from a particular point of view. Both are myths (though exaggerated in this case), constructed to understand and interpret true events and to help integrate those experiences into the larger stories we tell about ourselves and about our world. In order to make sense of our world, we repeat stories that contain meaning. Culture is made up of similar stories, which we choose in this work to call myths. We recognize, of course, that a common way that the term "myth" has been used is to refer to the false beliefs of another more "primitive" culture (Doty, 2004, p. 11). We would contend, however, that we all create and repeat myths that communicate meaning within our own cultures. A myth may be considered false, or it may communicate truth. However, what makes it a myth is its function as a carrier of meaning.

Myths, whether simple statements or complex stories, make claims about reality and constitute the lens through which a community forms identity. "A living myth expresses something fundamental about the worldview, values, and lifestyle of the people who accept it" (Chernus, 2012). Some examples of myths are as follows:

- Science is the path to a more utopian society.
- Religion is the cause of conflict in the world.
- There is no authority higher than the judgment of the community.
- There is no authority higher than the rule of law.
- Redistribution of wealth can solve the problems of our society.
- Private property is a basic human right.
- What goes around, comes around.
- Everything happens for a reason.

As we read this list of common everyday myths, we might find that some of them are embedded within our own assumptions. A myth, as a statement of culture, may be either true or false. Either way, it is a cultural story that conveys meaning. We live in the myths we tell because they are the stuff of culture. Some of these simple statements may have resonated with us, reflecting how we believe things should or do work. On the other hand, some in this same list may cause a visceral reaction against a particular statement. Some myths emerge from other cultures—even nearby cultures—and we find ourselves at odds with the claims or assumptions of a foreign perspective. Myths like those above are the building blocks of culture: They are the stories we tell about ourselves and the nature of our world. They have varying degrees of correspondence to truth, but are often more wrapped up in consolidating value and meaning in a manner which can be passed on and preserved generationally.

Why "Myths"?

In our cross-cultural training, we were taught to understand culture in terms of worldview. In this anthropological model, every culture is ascribed a particular framework that explains their unique values, beliefs, and experiences which affect the way they view their world (Kraft, 2008, pp. 75–128). Each culture or subculture will see the world through its own lens. The concept of worldview is a helpful resource as an anthropological base for ministering cross-culturally. Yet, in the context of cities populated by individuals and communities from several different nationalities, we want to expand our lens for viewing culture. We desire to look beyond the tendency to think of culture in terms of a monolithic reality or to interact with various members of a culture as if they share a uniform understanding of the world. When we first encounter a different culture, we may begin to understand a general worldview, including its values and practices, in new ways. The model below is helpful as a starting point (Hiebert, 2008, p. 26). Still, taking into account the regular cultural adaptations and exchanges occurring in our era of globalization and the development of multicultural neighborhoods, we want to push deeper in seeking effective ministry approaches in our multicultural encounters.

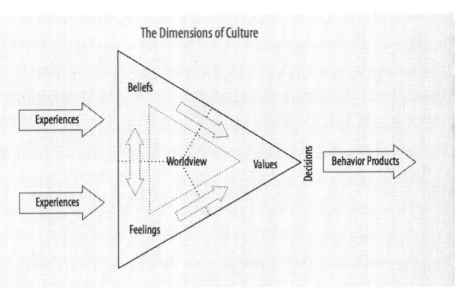

The way in which this worldview model tends to address culture is helpful when we are studying a majority culture as an outsider. It is an important starting point as it allows us to ask the initial questions we need to before gaining a deeper understanding of a particular culture. For example, how do the experiences of a particular people shape their understanding of the world around them? Furthermore, we may ask, what are the differences between how an honor-shame culture functions and the assumptions within a fear–power culture, or from the general perspectives of a culture that might be described as based in guilt–innocence (Georges, 2014)? In the multicultural city, we often find that a community we are seeking to reach actually represents multiple subcultures. In the past, the experience of many missionaries was to enter a single (traditional) culture, learn its ways, and contextualize the Gospel message for that particular people, but our mission fields are increasingly becoming places of expanding diversity. In a traditional homogenous culture, we may identify a single ethos saturating every aspect of the society, but in the diverse tapestry of the city, each cultural niche may have its own particular themes (McCurdy et al., 2004, pp. 77–78). Indeed, even in more traditional societies, it is certainly difficult to conclude that studying one cultural niche or community somehow sums up the total understanding of a people (Geertz, 1973, p. 22). Furthermore, in truly global settings it is common to find a collection of cultural threads representing a variety of subcultures braided together in a single community. Because they are naturally accustomed to functioning together within a high level of diversity, it is not surprising to find a well-connected community of individuals representing an array of cultural worldviews.

An important first step in cross-cultural ministry is to realize that not everyone sees the world as we do. Reaching out to diaspora communities, we may discover any number of worldviews, and assuming everyone thinks just like us or even like one another is shortsighted. Furthermore, as we encounter our diaspora neighbors, each subculture or microculture represents a specific worldview of its own, so it is important for the casual reader to guard against over-generalizing. Sometimes what appears to be a single cultural group to an outsider may actually represent several closely related—even interconnected—cultural threads within a diaspora community.

Once I (Jared) was starting a small house church in a Dominican home in New York City. There were no more than eight people in the room at any one gathering, yet the group represented at least three distinct cultural experiences. There were the middle-aged immigrants from professional backgrounds. There were the second generation pre-teen and teenage children who had grown up between cultures in New York City, and there were the twenty-something first generation immigrants who had quickly begun to assimilate and join the social grouping and activities of the second generation. Even in this small gathering of the same national origin, there were diverse cultural threads. At the same time, these differing cultural threads sharing many aspects of life together are often found within the same households. As ambassadors of the Gospel, we are addressing different cultures in cities that host growing diaspora communities from various parts of the world and in different stages of change and adaptation across multiple generations. Therefore, we want to help Christian leaders in North America share the simple message of the Gospel within this mosaic of cultures. Realizing the potential diversity of worldviews within the same city is an important first step in estimating cultural distinctives.

This work offers some approaches for interpreting culture that are decisive as ministers face two distinct realities in globalizing cities: (a) most of our friends and neighbors in the diaspora are in the process of assimilating and blending cultures, so their worldview is undergoing the sort of transition which makes it somewhat of a moving target; (b) the tendency of urban life is to create a myriad of subcultures, manifesting in many different ways and steadily increasing across North America. For this reason, we offer an approach for engaging the myriad of cultural perspectives that the average Christian leader is likely to encounter.

Our effort, here, is to present the models we use for analyzing and discussing the culturally fluid communities among which we minister. We feel that the language of "myth" allows us to discuss productively the diversity and dynamism of diaspora mission without over-generalizing. Often when we engage a specific culture as an outsider to that culture, it is easy for us to rush to apply a category as a definitive descriptor for the culture. We simply need a more adaptive approach. Applying the interpretive lens of myth allows the cross-cultural minister a theological grid through which to recognize how the Gospel intersects with the culture's narratives and to filter the ways different cultural transitions and accommodations interact as members of different cultural groups mingle in emerging communities.

For example, in one of the communities where we work, three primary leaders have been working with me (Seth) in reaching their neighborhood. All three come from the Bronx in New York, are Latino or Italian, and have been Christians for a similar length of time. We might tend to lump them together within the same worldview due to growing up in the same urban environment. When it comes to functioning as leaders, however, vastly disparate views began to emerge between them. One member came from a large church in the city that had been planted by his grandfather and is viewed within his community as an authority by way of inheritance. Even after leaving the faith for some years, when he returned to Christ, his status as an authority in that church was still intact based on his familial heritage. Another grew up as a Catholic and tends to see authority as linked to possessing specific offices or titles. Yet another has a highly charismatic faith and vests authority in those who are most certain that their ideas are Spirit-led. Both authors of this text tend to vest authority in personal ministry experience and education. These are only three leaders, trained and mentored in the same small group. Yet, despite sharing similar backgrounds in terms of a general cultural profile, they represent significant diversity within a shared community.

Any sub-cultures we could observe must take into account the differences of these leaders in conflict resolution, spiritual discernment, the place of religion in society, and many other issues. This is not just a matter of differing individual opinions. Indeed, this book is an effort to help Christian leaders interpret the inevitable differences they encounter as they reach out into diverse communities. We agree with Stewart and Bennett: "A deeper understanding of the nature of cultural differences would increase the effectiveness of Americans in cross-cultural situations" (Stewart & Bennett, 1991, p. x). Each of these individuals represents a larger network, within the same culture, which has adapted to particular experiences in order to maintain similar beliefs and values. In the age of "the global village," there is a need to push for dynamic frameworks for interpreting the varying cultural narratives that emerge within our ministries (Campbell, 1991). We believe these differences can be helpfully explained as different applications of shared myths.

This degree of diversity is true not only of multi-ethnic neighborhoods but to a surprising degree when reaching out to a single ethnic neighborhood in the city as well. We might ask, for example, why some people in a Muslim community appear to be religiously devoted while others seem highly secularized. Or why in a Latino community there are such strong cultural differences between those who migrated from *la ciudad* (the city) versus those who migrated from *el campo* (the country). We might ask: What differences exist between the more assimilated and those who more closely represent the homeland? What emerging subcultures are being generated by the second generation children of immigrant parents? Does this ethnic network expand across both urban density and suburban sprawl? These are only some of the questions we might ask as we encounter the variety of cultural threads intertwining within a diaspora community in a multicultural city.

In other words, to minister well in global cities, where so many cultures intersect to form communities, a nuanced understanding of culture is necessary to navigate the many ministerial issues that will emerge. To serve a multicultural community requires not only a basic grasp of culture, but also recognition of the interplay between cultures within the same community of faith.

A narrative approach is the most helpful starting place for leaders seeking to decipher cultural statements or behaviors they might encounter. We will use the term "myth" frequently throughout this work and with no intended commentary on the truth value of any particular cultural construct or assumption. Many individuals in our culture are under the impression that the term "myth" denotes something equivalent to a fantasy story. However, myths might be either true or false in their relationship to reality; this does not affect their status as myth. In scholarship those who study the concept of myth have observed a variety of definitions used differently in various contexts (Doty, 2004, pp. 1–30). Myth is a term we use to help us understand the *function* of a belief, not whether it is true or false.

We are aware of how the term "myth" has often been used in popular culture, but we find that the function of myth is an effective way to understand culture. Mythic models, as we hope to demonstrate, create an approach as dynamic as the dizzying mix of coexisting cultures we encounter in the context of multicultural cities throughout North America. The function of myths is to encapsulate truths, values, or ideas in a way that can adapt to changes in culture over time without losing the value or belief in question. Put another way, one scholar explains, "Typically, myths provide symbolic representations of cultural priorities, beliefs, and prejudices....myths coalesce social values or projections that have been found worthy of repetition and replication" (Doty, 2004, pp. 18–20). Myth is the stuff of culture. Understanding culture through myths provides a broad lens for seeing culture through a narrative framework. Myths describe worldviews, represent shared values, and explain lifestyles within a culture (Chernus, 2012). Each of us as authors hold some myths to be true, but at the same time recognize them as myths in the way they function. By "myth" we simply mean the larger narratives which constitute a particular cultural identity and which serve as lenses through which a given people view and interpret their experiences.

For the duration of this work, then, we will describe "culture" as "the shared myths within a people group, and the relationships and learned behaviors that emerge from those myths." Additionally, we will use the term "narrative" to mean "the assumptions that stem from and demonstrate the working out of cultural myths." All cultures and individuals operate in the realm of myth and narratives; this assertion is not meant to be understood with any sense of superiority or paternalism. We are not in the business of passing broad judgments on cultures. All cultures must answer to the Gospel and are also available as vehicles for understanding the Gospel. When we encounter a new subculture in any of our cities, it is important to remember that the culture we are encountering will have inherent bridges for communicating the Gospel as well as inherent barriers to the Gospel. No worldview is unbroken by sin nor is any culture too lost to be included in the reconciling work of God. When we encounter a particular community or reach out to our new neighbors from another part of the world, we should ask ourselves, "What am I observing that represents a bridge for the Gospel, and what am I observing that represents a real barrier for the Gospel?"

Globalization and Urbanization

One of the key reasons for the existence of this book is to help equip those Christian leaders without a prior background in cross-cultural studies to face confidently the twin realities of globalization and urbanization that results in so many people from such different cultural backgrounds co-existing in close proximity and interacting with one another in a metropolitan region. Our world is shrinking. The challenges facing contemporary ministries are significant, and the opportunities are unprecedented. "The number of people moving from their respective homelands to other countries or from one place to another is growing" (Im & Casiño, 2014, p. 6), and mobility is a key factor impacting our local contexts for ministry. Furthermore, it is likely to continue to impact evangelism strategies going forward. At least twenty cities across the globe now boast populations of more than one million residents who were born in a foreign nation (Price & Benton-Short, January 1, 2007). Christian churches in the United States will continue to find themselves confronted with the challenge of cross-cultural mission in their own backyard, as people from around the world continue to migrate to American cities—both the central city and the surrounding suburbs and edge cities. In fact, immigrants in the United States represent 20% of the world's migrants (Payne, 2012, p. 40).

Over one million new immigrants arrive in the United States every year—a trend likely to continue. While the Hispanic population in the United States has surpassed that of African-Americans, Asian communities actually represent the fastest growing ethnic communities in the country (Im & Casiño, 2014). Despite real challenges, we believe that the church in North America is witnessing unprecedented opportunities at its doorstep. We realize, however, that Christian leaders will need guidance and helpful resources to navigate the new world we now face together. In many respects, this global migration has changed the makeup of American cities to such an extent that it demands a revisiting of our contemporary distinction between foreign missions and local ministry. Rather than crossing an ocean, many leaders and churches will need to become equipped as cross-cultural missionaries in order to simply cross the street or drive across town as ambassadors of the Gospel. The reality of globalization is having a profound impact on the church and its mission. "In a world of instant global communication and jet travel, time and space shrink and force a new awareness upon all the inhabitants of the earth" (Esposito, Fasching, & Lewis, 2007, p. 3).

In our society it is often the case that "globalization" is heard as a political term or as something that we are supposed to be either for or against. However, in this work, we do not view the term "globalization" as a political statement. It is simply a reality of contemporary ministry, and for this reason, we will speak of globalization in largely neutral terms. Regardless of how it makes us feel, globalized communities *are* the context for contemporary ministry in our cities. Injustices are inherent in the trends and activities associated with globalization because those injustices flow out of the condition of human societies. Opportunities for the Gospel flow out of the trends and activities of globalization because God is at work in our world and His Kingdom advances through incarnational means. "Globalization is not just an economic matter but is concerned with issues of cultural meaning. While the values and meanings attached to place remain significant, we are increasingly involved in networks which extend far beyond our immediate physical location" (Barker, 2003, p. 169). These realities of our global world embody unprecedented opportunities for the mission of the church. However, Christian ministries must also learn to navigate the enormous challenges as well. Globalization is our context for ministry among the nations as men and women from around the world establish families, start businesses, and build communities in cities far from the nation of their birth. As cities act as magnets for international migration, local ministry contexts are increasingly impacted by global currents. In many cities, a drive across a single metropolitan region should be enough to convince us that we are all truly missionaries now.

These global trends have a significant impact upon the ministry of the local church. Globalization means that increasing numbers of people are on the move. Urbanization means that diverse groups of people are drawn into close proximity. Coupled together, this high rate of global mobility with close proximity presents a new mission field for the local church in metropolitan areas across North America. It also means that the church will be compelled to respond with more than a one-size-fits-all approach. There will be a need for mono-cultural ethnic churches among immigrants who have recently arrived in their host city as well as hybrid, multicultural churches that exist at the intersection of cultures (Leonard, January 1, 2004).

In the past, ministers in suburban churches have viewed their church as outside of the reach of urban life and culture with the exception of short-term ministry excursions. This is no longer the case, as it is becoming increasingly apparent with a simple stroll through the mall, that globalization is not limited to the inner city. In addition, there is a need for a fresh perspective on the ecology of cities. Today, many cities should be understood as expansive and multi-centered metropolitan areas. Contemporary cities are multidimensional. Center city and suburban neighborhoods are linked to urban culture, although in different ways, and participate in the fabric of the city's life and customs. Some church leaders may read this book from their office at the end of the hall in a suburban church building sitting a few blocks from an interstate highway. While it once required a forty-five-minute drive downtown to engage in cross-cultural ministry through the local mission partner, now nearby multiethnic neighborhoods, apartment complexes drawing from the populations of refugee resettlements, ethnic markets, and immigrant associations are transforming the fabric of their suburban community and increasing the social links between ethnic communities across their metro region.

A binary view of the city as suburban or inner city no longer accurately reflects the cultural landscape of cities. The world has become a smaller place while the city has become a bigger place. Cities are much more expansive and multi-centered. For congregational leaders and church planters, cross-cultural ministry has become a local activity. Globalization and urbanization are not far-off concepts affecting simply a handful of urban ministers, but rather cross-cultural ministry has come into close proximity for an increasing number of American churches scattered across metropolitan regions.

Diaspora

The term diaspora, originally describing communities of Jews scattered across the Mediterranean world during the Roman Empire, is increasingly used to describe numerous cultures that are relocating and establishing new ethnic communities around the world (Cohen, 1997, pp. 21–22). Today, global migration is a common occurrence and cities throughout North America increasingly represent international populations. Like many readers of this book, we believe this is an extraordinary opportunity for the mission of the church. Throughout this book, we will refer to the various cultural or immigrant communities that we encounter in our cities as our "diaspora" neighbors. We hope to be constantly reminded to love our neighbors who have arrived from various nations around the world.

When addressing cross-cultural outreach in diaspora communities, we use this description as a broad sweep across a cultural group. As Christian leaders make strides in reaching out to nearby diaspora communities, they often encounter a spectrum of cultural adaptations to the new host society on the one hand and on the other, attempts to retain cultural ideas, customs, and myths from the sending country. Culture in the city is in a constant state of retention, adaptation, and assimilation.

When churches begin serving a diaspora community in a North American city, they will likely encounter first generation immigrants who have arrived in recent weeks, months, or years as well as the second generation of a diaspora community. The second generation consists of the children of migrants and are often bilingual. They are partly at home in the diaspora community and partly at home in the wider American culture, though not feeling completely at home in either. While the second generation may be culturally similar to their parents, they still represent distinct cultures and subcultures that require churches to think cross-culturally. Our experience, in fact, has shown that the second generation's culture is often the most complex. Second generation residents of diaspora communities navigate both cultural worlds fluently but also form hybrid cultures of their own, blending the values of both inherited contexts. In addition, cross-cultural evangelists may encounter a third generation emerging from the diaspora community. They often have lost the ability to speak their grandparents' language, are much more at home in the broader culture of American society, but may maintain certain myths and other components of their grandparents' culture that inform their identity and sense of heritage.

The Gospel

Perhaps it seems unnecessary to define the Gospel, but in our experience it is the undefined that causes us to misunderstand and to talk past one another. When we read the accounts of Jesus's life in the four Gospels, we see that he preached the "good news" about the Kingdom of God. Likewise, where the book of Acts leaves off with Paul's final journey, he is in Rome teaching about the Kingdom of God which has now been revealed more fully through the death and resurrection of Christ. We thus interpret evangelism to include a variety of topics and teachings about what it means for God's reign to be realized the lives of the people in a particular cultural context. While proclaiming the death and resurrection are crucial components of the Gospel, they are a part of the larger story of God's Kingdom breaking into human existence. The cross and the resurrection are certainly the central climax of the Gospel, and simultaneously they are pointing to the larger reality of the Gospel—the redemptive reign of God.

In other words, we find that no retelling of the Gospel is complete without the revelation of Christ's divinity, passion, and his resurrection, but neither does the retelling of those points without a wider message of God's reign, Jesus's teaching, and continuing mission constitute a full picture of the Gospel. For instance, a person may hear the message of Jesus's loving and painful sacrifice, but if that is the only Gospel presentation they ever hear, they miss out on Jesus's call to discipleship, the importance of the "one another" commands that make up the building blocks of Christian community, or the world-changing challenge of loving our enemies. Therefore, a single event of sharing the Gospel is often one brushstroke of a larger portrait of God's work of salvation and justice. That does not mean we should be overzealous and overload our hearers with every aspect of the Gospel in one sitting. That is unlikely to be helpful. Rather, in every story we share we are pointing to God's redemptive reign through Jesus Christ. Clearly, some stories are more central to the Gospel than others, but every opportunity to point to God's Kingdom is a step in the right direction and constitutes sharing the good news.

In our work, we often think of evangelization as similar to creating a mosaic that will depict God and God's Kingdom. Evangelism is the casting of a vision to make God visible to a culture or a community. At the center of the picture is Jesus: his life, death, and resurrection. Throughout the process of building the full picture many little pieces must be added as the work of the Gospel presses into deeper chambers of one's heart. As the mosaic of the Gospel becomes more complete in a person's vision, it expounds on and challenges any number of issues common across our human experience, such as race, money, power, poverty, sexuality, violence, and community. The multifaceted interaction of the Gospel message with these issues forms pieces of the larger picture of God's reign. Any time we bring the Gospel to bear on concerns like these, we help add a piece to the complete picture of God and thus, do the work of evangelism. We are literally "good-newsing." At the same time, we have not fully shared the Gospel with someone until there is a clear enough picture for them to recognize who it is a picture of, a point unreachable without the centrality of the cross.

Cultural Backdrops

If someone moves deeply into conversation with an individual or group from a strikingly different culture, it is not unusual to walk away from the dialog thinking, "How can they think that?" When a missionary enters a culture half a world away from her home, she has to use a different set of lenses to decipher what is occurring from the viewpoint of the host culture. When we begin working cross-culturally—even close to home—it is helpful factors to realize that a different set of cultural backdrops may be at work. We have found that the *3D Gospel*, by Jayson Georges, is a helpful resource for introducing American Christians to some common cultural patterns that we might encounter when working with different cultures. It is an accessible starting point for recognizing the realities of different cultural worlds.

Georges divides the world into three cultural types. First, there is "guilt and innocence." This worldview appears to be quite common among Westerners. It is individualistic in perspective and focuses on a clear sense of absolute right or wrong. A second cultural type is "fear and power." This perspective prevails among those who view reality as the playing out of different spiritual forces and the manipulation of invisible powers. The Gospel of Mark appears to address this framework frequently as Jesus demonstrates total authority over the powers of the spiritual realm and of nature. Third, there is "honor and shame." This view might be contrasted to some degree with the notion of guilt and innocence because we are less focused on the individual's relationships with their own actions but are heavily invested in the impact his or her actions have upon the group with whom they most identify. The Bible frequently addresses issues associated with honor and shame, especially as these issues play out often in more communal cultures (Georges, 2014).

While this is a helpful starting point for learning about differing cultural perspectives, we would like to warn against slapping a singular label of any one category on a cultural group. For instance, you may encounter a cultural group that represents a strong honor-shame dynamic in their everyday interactions; however, after spending more time with the community, you may discover an additional layer of fear–power at work. These categories are not so much singular compartments for various cultures as they are dimensions of culture that reflect the ways groups interact with one another and the world around them. When crossing cultures, it is generally wise to refrain from rushing to judgment but to take time to learn the varying dimensions at work within a cultural community.

As Christian leaders cross cultural barriers as messengers of the Gospel, they are likely to encounter these different cultural backdrops that inform decision-making, people's perceptions, and even how they will hear and interpret the stories of the Bible. It is important to remember that some of the cultures we are reaching in our cities come from a cultural world closer to that of the setting of the Bible than our own. Forgetting this fact might cause us to leap to unnecessary conclusions influenced more by our own cultural background than the actual biblical story. Our diaspora neighbors are often a rich blessing as they accompany us through reading Scripture and applying biblical actions. It is not uncommon in our experience for the evangelist to become the student as we have the opportunity to process fresh perspectives from our international friends. The Christian church is truly global when each community in their own cultural context are able to work out the expression of the Gospel that makes sense to their families and neighbors and when culturally different communities are able to function as equals in the faith and offer one another theological critique (Ezigbo & Williams, 2014, p. 101).

Furthermore, it is important to remember that in a diaspora setting, we are likely to encounter any variety of hybrids. Many people have been exposed to several competing myths, worldviews, cultures, and traditions. Therefore, they may exhibit a combination of these that otherwise, in a more homogenous cultural setting, would seem contradictory and unproductive. Evangelists in diaspora communities, particularly where individuals and families are simultaneously seeking to retain their culture of origin and experiencing varying degrees of assimilation, will need to listen well in order to determine what cultural backdrops are influencing their hearers.

Contextualization

Evangelism must begin with us. It is our responsibility to see that our communication of the message speaks effectively to the cultures of others. We see the clearest model of this principle in Jesus, who incarnated himself fully into the forms, structures, and myths of first century Palestine in order to communicate the Gospel. As we continue reading in Acts, the early apostles adapted their proclamation of the Gospel based on whether they were speaking to a Greek audience or a Jewish audience. Naturally, the particular theological and ethical issues in a specific instance that are addressed in our Bibles at times varied whether the evangelist was addressing pagans, Jews, or God-fearing Greeks. The early Christian leaders in our New Testament narratives and letters naturally understood the nuances of culture as they lived in a region that experienced one of the earliest forms of globalization under the imposition of the Roman Empire. The early church was full of diaspora missionaries.

Following Jesus's incarnational example, we too seek to enter as fully as possible into the culture and myths of our diaspora neighbors, *becoming all things to all people* (1 Cor. 9:22–23) in order to communicate the message of the Kingdom in every context. This is most often called contextualization; that is, the Gospel of Christ operating within a particular cultural context. The central message of the Gospel is constant, but the Gospel may be embodied within a host of cultures and expressions. If we fail to recognize the role of culture, we might be blind to the impact of our own culture in our understanding or application of the Gospel.

When working cross-culturally, it is important to grasp the basic concept of contextualization. As an ambassador of the Gospel to my neighbors from other nations, I want to communicate the message as responsibly as I can. I desire them to understand the thrust of the message and be able to wrestle with its implications within their own cultural arena. As they become followers of Jesus, I hope to teach them in such a way that they can share the message of Christ clearly with their own family, friends, and neighbors in a manner that they too can understand and embrace within their own cultural world. In this way, most contextualization will and should take place between cultural insiders. In other words, we need to find ways for those who know their culture best to flesh out the Gospel within their cultural world. However, in order to contextualize the greater arc of the Gospel our cross-cultural friends must first hear it in a form they can interpret. Each culture has its own inherent bridges and barriers to the Gospel. If I assume that my own concerns, customs, ideas, prejudices, etc. are automatically aligned with those of different cultural backgrounds, I assume too much and may talk right past them. Therefore, we need to learn to listen well so that we can be effective messengers of the Gospel across cultural divides—even those that occur within geographic proximity.

As we consider crossing cultures as messengers of the Gospel, we certainly want to encourage thinking critically and creatively about how we carry the Gospel into another cultural context. In order to do this well, we want to offer two ways of thinking about contextualization. The Gospel is embodied through the expressions and concepts of a culture, and it also challenges the fallen aspects of a culture from within. This contextualization takes two forms: formal and conceptual.

Formal Contextualization

Formal contextualization deals with what forms social relationships take in culture. It is essentially guided by the question: How do people communicate here? Formal contextualization may relate to the *method of communication*: When people interact in normal relationships, do they tell stories? Are parables recognized and understood? How common are proverbs, and what status do they hold in relationship to wisdom? Does this culture have songs that are commonly known and are invested with meaning? Is debate the primary means of discussing truth? How does religion interface with technology? In other words, how do people communicate with one another within a culture when it comes to matters of great importance or meaning? These are the types of questions we want to explore when discerning the best manner or form for proclaiming the good news.

Formal contextualization also may pertain to *vocabulary*. For example, it is probably best when working with Muslims to use the Arabic terms: *Allah* for God, *Isa* for Jesus, and *Injil* for Gospel. When working with anyone raised outside of Christendom we need to be careful to avoid using technical theological language or "church-speak" which generally tends to be "insider" vocabulary and is not obvious to those not already familiar with the concepts. It may also be helpful to

47

keep in mind the political implications of terms with which we are already quite comfortable. For instance, our team realized early on that using the word "Christian" to describe ourselves may not always be the best option with Muslims because, in some Islamic cultures, the term "Christian" suggests an immoral person. From this vantage point, Americans are seen as immoral; if the United States has a "Christian" culture, then Christians must be immoral as well. True, the term "Christian" is found in the Bible, and we believe it is a good word. Still, in these situations we often refer to ourselves as "followers of Isa" (Jesus) to avoid misperceptions while still expressing our allegiance to Christ.

Formal contextualization may also deal with the *social structures of culture*: Is it appropriate for men to speak to women who are not family in a public setting or vice versa? Should adults pay less attention to children in a social setting or give extra honor to the elderly? What does a spiritual person look like in this culture? One of our co-workers in the city came back from visiting his family and was told by his African Muslim friends that they could no longer trust his teachings about Jesus. When questioned, they said that everyone knows that religious teachers have beards; he had shaved off his beard while he was away seeking financial partners. To them, returning without a beard indicated that he was no longer a religious teacher. Many such elements must be considered in formal contextualization.

Conceptual Contextualization

Conceptual contextualization, as the name suggests, concerns adapting concepts in order to speak to culture. Do analogies exist in this culture to help explain the atonement? Is sin understood as shame, guilt, or being under the authority of demonic powers? How politically charged is language like "justification" or "liberation?" When hearing the Gospel, people of different cultures and subcultures interpret the message through different mythic frameworks and respond with questions that emerge from highly disparate understandings and values.

For example, in Bangladeshi culture, the Hindu minority has little difficulty understanding the notion of our belief in the Trinity, although it may seem to them that our belief confirms their own polytheism. Discussions with Hindus, then, may deal frequently with the supreme lordship of Jesus over other gods. The first stages of evangelism are often an effort to elevate Jesus above the pantheon, in a similar way that the Old Testament narratives elevate the Lord above all other "gods." In contrast, to speak about Jesus this way to the Muslim majority would immediately discredit the messenger. With Muslims it is probably best to demonstrate Jesus's authority as a prophet and interpreter of the law—similar to the depiction of Jesus we see in Matthew. Islam already contains a mythic structure that accepts the role of prophets and law as well as direct references to Jesus in the Qur'an. However, Hindus care nothing about the authority of these offices but highly value the mythic role of "guru" and "spiritual guide."

An evangelist may enter a predominantly South Asian neighborhood in an American city where Hindus and Muslims live next door to each other and work in the same businesses; however, the way one presents the Gospel of the Kingdom to a Hindu is often quite different than a conversation with a Muslim even from the same country of origin and living in the same diaspora community. Just as the early Apostles contextualized their Gospel presentations to different audiences, depending on whether they might be Jewish or Greek, we should expect to do the same in the various diaspora communities we encounter.

I (Jared) remember overhearing a discussion a group of Christian teenagers were having with a Muslim exchange student. The Christian teens meant well. They zealously attempted to witness to their Muslim peer. However, they completely bypassed the most natural bridge they already had in common—their shared belief in God. After they repeatedly challenged her for what they perceived as not believing in God, she became frustrated and raised her voice, saying, "I believe in God. Why do you keep saying, 'I don't believe in God?!'" They meant well, but their starting point ended up negating their good intentions and alienating their Muslim acquaintance from continued discussion of religious matters. Recognizing a common starting point may have led to a much more fruitful discussion.

While we want every new disciple to grow increasingly into a fuller and deeper understanding of the Gospel, every culture or subculture will have its own starting point. The question we must ask, then, is what are the initial bridges between their existing beliefs and the Gospel of Christ? Recognizing those cultural bridges allows the Christian witness to begin on common ground as the starting point for communicating the good news.

Conceptual contextualization is the most difficult; but also the most essential form of contextualization. We must be able to tell the story of Jesus in ways that can be understood and are relevant to our diaspora neighbor's culture; but, in doing so, we cannot sacrifice the integrity of the message and slip into syncretism. The intention of this book is to offer real guidance and tools for learning about the different cultures in our cities and to assist in making strategic ministry decisions for the sake of reaching further into that cultural group with the message of Christ.

A Word of Caution

There are two primary dangers in contextualization. The first danger is in believing that we, as missionaries, have as deep an understanding of the culture as the insiders of that culture, or that we can fully enter into and identify with the culture to the point of attaining insider status. Though Jesus is our model for cross-cultural ministry, we are not able to incarnate ourselves into a new people the way he did. It is arrogant to assume that we can ever truly shed our own cultural baggage or that we can fully take on the culture of another. This arrogance can lead us to believe that we know exactly how the Gospel should be heard in this culture and can decide for the culture how the Gospel should be interpreted and applied, treating our neighbor like they are not fit to hear the word and understand for themselves. This is more in keeping with paternalistic colonialism than the humility demonstrated by Jesus. We cannot hear the Gospel for another culture and we cannot decide for a people how they must respond. At our best, we can deliver the message with attempts to move it outside of our own cultural context and into forms and structures that will allow them a fair hearing of the Gospel. This is not, however, the same as telling them how to interpret or respond to the Gospel. We must always admit how limited we are in contextualizing the Gospel fully.

The other danger is in deluding ourselves about our ability to share the Gospel in a way that is neutral or outside of culture. No

51

person ever steps completely outside of culture, and the Gospel itself represents good news proclaimed within specific cultures. Being aware of our limitations will assist us in crossing cultures sensitively. In reading the four Gospels, we see four different accounts of Jesus as adapted to different community contexts, but in each case we encounter Jesus and the Kingdom of God as enculturated concepts. It is the duty of the missionary, then, to be aware of how inescapable culture is in relation to how we might interpret and proclaim the Gospel. We cannot simply tell the story of the good news and not acknowledge that our own understanding and our particular retelling of it are affected by our own cultural background. As a result, we should be prepared to ask questions and listen attentively to the perspectives of others, rather than to assume the accuracy of our own understanding.

In our work we use Discovery Bible Study (DBS) methods and inductive teaching styles—examples of which may be found in the appendices of this book—to minimize the degree to which the Gospel is communicated through the missionary rather than through the Scriptures themselves (Watson & Watson, 2014, 141–153). In this way, we are seeking to maximize the potential for new believers to express the Gospel in ways that make sense within their own cultural circles. Even so, we are only able to enter into the inductive study of Scripture after identifying spiritually interested people in the community through sharing our faith. It is especially vital in this initial sharing—as we communicate about Jesus before an individual has decided to engage with Scripture—that we are aware of how great our duty is to think in terms of contextualization. Even the decision to evangelize through an inductive, discovery-based, teaching style is a decision regarding contextualization.

One of the reasons we prefer a discovery approach is that it creates space for our diaspora friends to begin giving shape to the expression of the Gospel within their culture or subculture. However, when we determine which Bible passages constitute an effective Bible study series, we are making a contextualization decision because we are choosing in advance passages we believe will best communicate the message of Christ to a particular audience. It is helpful to acknowledge these nuances when crossing into a culture different from our own. For every testimony we share, every story we choose to tell or not to tell, every section of Scripture we choose to study or not to study, we as missionaries are making judgments about Gospel and culture: We are making decisions about contextualization. To fail to acknowledge this is to choose to keep the message contextualized within our own culture, and as a result, we may end up communicating the Gospel in a way that is foreign to the hearer while quite comfortable to our own ears. The key step is to communicate in ways people understand, minimize the impact of our own cultural assumptions, and see believers in Christ begin to express the truth of the Gospel in ways that makes sense to their cultural peers.

Practice

Identifying Contextualization in Scripture

Read the following sermons from Acts and identify the ways that Paul and Peter have adapted their messages respective to their audiences. Pay particular attention to the ways they choose to employ Scripture or not, and the roles in which they depict God and Jesus in relationship to their hearers' religious cultural frameworks.

Acts 2:14–36 (NRSV)

4 But Peter, standing with the eleven, raised his voice and addressed them, "Men of Judea and all who live in Jerusalem, let this be known to you, and listen to what I say. **15** Indeed, these are not drunk, as you suppose, for it is only nine o'clock in the morning. **16** No, this is what was spoken through the prophet Joel: **17** 'In the last days it will be, God declares, that I will pour out my Spirit upon all flesh, and your sons and your daughters shall prophesy, and your young men shall see visions, and your old men shall dream dreams. **18** Even upon my slaves, both men and women, in those days I will pour out my Spirit; and they shall prophesy. **19** And I will show portents in the heaven above and signs on the earth below, blood, and fire, and smoky mist. **20** The sun shall be turned to darkness and the moon to blood, before the coming of the Lord's great and glorious day. **21** Then everyone who calls on the name of the Lord shall be saved.' **22** "You that are Israelites, listen to what I have to say: Jesus of Nazareth, a man attested to you by God with deeds of power, wonders, and signs that God did through him among you, as you yourselves know— **23** this man, handed over to you according to the definite plan and foreknowledge of God, you crucified and killed by the hands of those

54

outside the law. **24** But God raised him up, having freed him from death, because it was impossible for him to be held in its power. **25** For David says concerning him, 'I saw the Lord always before me, for he is at my right hand so that I will not be shaken; **26** therefore my heart was glad, and my tongue rejoiced; moreover my flesh will live in hope. **27** For you will not abandon my soul to Hades, or let your Holy One experience corruption. **28** You have made known to me the ways of life; you will make me full of gladness with your presence.' **29** "Fellow Israelites, I may say to you confidently of our ancestor David that he both died and was buried, and his tomb is with us to this day. **30** Since he was a prophet, he knew that God had sworn with an oath to him that he would put one of his descendants on his throne. **31** Foreseeing this, David spoke of the resurrection of the Messiah, saying, 'He was not abandoned to Hades, nor did his flesh experience corruption.' **32** This Jesus God raised up, and of that all of us are witnesses. **33** Being therefore exalted at the right hand of God, and having received from the Father the promise of the Holy Spirit, he has poured out this that you both see and hear. **34** For David did not ascend into the heavens, but he himself says, 'The Lord said to my Lord, 'Sit at my right hand, **35** until I make your enemies your footstool.'"**36** Therefore let the entire house of Israel know with certainty that God has made him both Lord and Messiah, this Jesus whom you crucified."

Notes:

Acts 17:16–31 (NRSV)

6 While Paul was waiting for them in Athens, he was deeply distressed to see that the city was full of idols. **17** So he argued in the synagogue with the Jews and the devout persons, and also in the marketplace every day with those who happened to be there. **18** Also some Epicurean and Stoic philosophers debated with him. Some said, "What does this babbler want to say?" Others said, "He seems to be a proclaimer of foreign divinities." (This was because he was telling the good news about Jesus and the resurrection.) **19** So they took him and brought him to the Areopagus and asked him, "May we know what this new teaching is that you are presenting? **20** It sounds rather strange to us, so we would like to know what it means." **21** Now all the Athenians and the foreigners living there would spend their time in nothing but telling or hearing something new. **22** Then Paul stood in front of the Areopagus and said, "Athenians, I see how extremely religious you are in every way. **23** For as I went through the city and looked carefully at the objects of your worship, I found among them an altar with the inscription, 'To an unknown god.' What therefore you worship as unknown, this I proclaim to you. **24** The God who made the world and everything in it, he who is Lord of heaven and earth, does not live in shrines made by human hands, **25** nor is he served by human hands, as though he needed anything, since he himself gives to all mortals life and breath and all things. **26** From one ancestor he made all nations to inhabit the whole earth, and he allotted the times of their existence and the boundaries of the places where they would live, **27** so that they would search for God and perhaps grope for him and find him—though indeed he is not far from each one of us.**28** For 'In him we live and move and have our being'; as even some of your own poets have said,

'For we too are his offspring.' **29** Since we are God's offspring, we ought not to think that the deity is like gold, or silver, or stone, an image formed by the art and imagination of mortals. **30** While God has overlooked the times of human ignorance, now he commands all people everywhere to repent, **31** because he has fixed a day on which he will have the world judged in righteousness by a man whom he has appointed, and of this he has given assurance to all by raising him from the dead."

Notes:

Section One

Foundational Tools for Entering Cross-Cultural Ministry

To enter cross-cultural ministry is to become a learner. We are stepping into a cultural world not our own. Fortunately, the Gospel provides a foundation for entering culture: "The Word became flesh and dwelled among us" (John 1:14). Jesus entered a specific cultural context where he put the good news of God's mission into terms that both embraced and challenged the cultures around him. This taking on and entering into of history and culture is an essential part of God becoming flesh; in our work we talk about ministry built on this principle as being "incarnational" work. We find this same incarnational quality in the work of the apostle Paul as he followed Jesus's model of bringing good news across cultural barriers. For years, missionaries have followed in the footsteps of the forerunners of their faith as they crossed cultural barriers and called those who are different from themselves, "brother" and "sister." As our cities become increasingly diverse places welcoming nations from around the globe, ministries that once assumed a degree of homogeneity can no longer afford to do so. In center cities and sprawling suburbs we are all missionaries now; therefore, we must begin to learn the tools of the trade.

In the following chapters we will introduce some essential practices needed to be a learner about other cultures. Two key skills that have been utilized by anthropologists and missionaries for many years are ethnographic interviewing and participant observation. Put simply, we want to learn to ask good questions and to become attentive and intentional observers of what is taking place around us. The more we learn about another's culture, the more effectively we can consciously move beyond our own cultural presuppositions and communicate clearly to our diaspora neighbors.

As we make discoveries about the cultures of our diaspora neighbors, we begin to understand who they are as people within God's creation. As individuals and families come into relationship with the transforming power of the Gospel, issues of cultural identity that might otherwise be taken for granted often rise to the surface, and we celebrate that the Gospel can be embodied within each and every culture in our world. Contemporary missionaries have been grappling with aspects of cultural identity for decades. In an increasingly diverse global society, cultural identity is multifaceted, sometimes fluid, and even interconnected. Often, our diaspora neighbors' cultural identities are in the process of adapting to a dizzying array of new challenges as a result of migrating across national borders and outside of their cultural home. As cross-cultural workers in multicultural cities, the people we work with are anything but one-dimensional. In a global society, we are students of culture in a sea of change and diversity,

Leaders are tasked with facilitating a ministry's strategic vision. As globalization and urbanization transform metropolitan regions into vast cultural mosaics, our strategic options are many. While there is an urgent need for contextualized church planting, there is much that existing churches can do within their present capacities and resources. We want to emphasize the importance for ministry leaders to think creatively and contextually and to avoid prescriptive solutions; however, we do want to offer some basic frameworks for thinking about outreach strategies in increasingly diverse metropolitan areas. Throughout this book, we reflect upon cross-cultural experiences that might at times stretch the imagination of those who have largely remained confined with their own cultural boundaries. We hope sharing these missionary practices and cross-cultural stories will provide a starting point as Christian leaders begin stepping into contexts that may be geographically near, yet feel culturally a world away.

Chapter 2

Becoming a Student of Culture

A minister of a local church in a small city begins building relationships with international refugees in a nearby community. He becomes friends with men and their families from Syria, Iraq, Somalia, and Bhutan. He deeply desires to share the Gospel with his new neighbors and hopes to see them place their faith in Christ, yet he has no previous training in cross-cultural ministry and is not sure where to begin. A church elder has noticed that the signs in his local supermarket are beginning to appear in Spanish as well as English, but he has not built many relationships with these new neighbors yet. He would like to be used as an evangelist, but he, too, is not sure where to begin.

The leaders of a local church in an old downtown neighborhood notice that the demographics of their surrounding community are transitioning. In the commercial areas surrounding their church building there are now shops advertising in Chinese, Arabic, and Spanish, and the nearby residential community is emerging as a multiethnic neighborhood. They have begun to initiate outreach to the community, but after several months of friendly neighborliness, an active food pantry program, and lots of neighborhood advertising, they have become discouraged. They have not seen any new members added to their church from the local community, and they are beginning to wonder what they are doing wrong.

Another church in the suburbs of a large metro area begins to experience growth and increasing diversity in their membership. For years, the lead pastor had dreamed of leading a more diverse assembly. As non-Western Christians from Nigeria, Ghana, and Central America moved into the community, the church welcomed them with open arms and made adjustments to worship styles and programming to make them feel warmly welcome. It was an exciting time for this church. However, recently the church leadership has begun to realize some nearby apartment complexes have filled up with Muslim immigrants from North Africa and the Middle East as well as Buddhists from Southeast Asian. The church feels compelled to find ways to reach these newest neighbors with the Gospel. They have attempted campaigns inviting them to church services, but this has not resulted in any new visitors from these culturally and religiously distant communities. Still, they are committed to finding a way to make an impact for the Gospel in these communities.

When missionaries are trained to cross cultures as messengers of the Gospel, they should begin to learn some key research tools to help them understand the cultural and religious contexts that they are now encountering. It is often important for missionaries to learn a new set of skills for encountering different cultures as an ambassador of the Gospel (Luzbetak, 2015, pp. 8–11). Upon first entering a new culture, good missionaries begin to practice "ethnography." Ethnography is what we do when we begin learning about a culture and become able to describe its traits. These skills are commonly adapted from cultural anthropology and used by cross-cultural missionaries. It is essential for missionaries to learn to listen well to the culture that is now hosting them. While there are some stark differences between living in a traditional society a world away from one's home and engaging a culturally different neighborhood a few miles away, consistently there are some key research practices that can help inform more effective ministry choices.

Whenever we take the step of crossing cultures to relate to others, we must learn to be good listeners. The missionary practice of ethnographic research is to seek clarity of understanding so that they can communicate the Gospel clearly and develop disciples and leaders who will faithfully embody the Gospel within their own culture. Whether we are integrating new Christian immigrants into our existing church body or going into a new ethnic community for the first time as church planters and evangelists, we need to learn to listen to others' stories and identify the bridges and barriers to the Gospel within their culture. "A key element in using ethnography as a pastoral practice is that it becomes a form of pastoral listening" (Moschella, 2008, p. 12). Learning to listen and grow in our ability to communicate effectively across cultures is an expression of love demonstrated to those who are distinctly different from us. As we minister to those culturally different from us, we enter the relationship as learners.

We might try to preach the Gospel to a particular ethnic community, but the manner through which we explain the Gospel might as well be in a language completely foreign to them —even if they speak English—if we do not realize how they might hear or interpret our words. We might try to initiate an event or program designed to serve a particular ethnic neighborhood, but how do we know if we are offering something that meets the most pressing needs of that community? We might offer a service to a particular ethnic neighborhood and feel like we are successful because many people are served, but how should we interpret the mysterious absence of the community's most important leaders when they are usually present for the most important community events in their neighborhood? There are no simple answers to these questions; the answers may be quite different depending on the particular people, context, and unique circumstances in each specific instance. Nevertheless, as ambassadors for Christ among the various cultures in our cities, we can begin to learn some key practices that will help us to ask the right questions in order to discover more effective ways to connect with our new neighbors from around the globe. As we encounter various communities in our city, "the goal of the researcher is to see the world through the eyes of the culture under study" (Wan & Casey, 2014, p. 63). Although we can never fully enter the culture of another, we can identify key bridges and help coach new believers as they become carriers of the Gospel message within their own culture.

In this chapter we will survey some basic practices utilized by missionary anthropologists, and discuss how you might implement the basics of these practices to discern the most effective and responsible approaches to carry out ministry among a specific people or community. Doing research in a community by applying these practices "is a way of immersing yourself in the life of a people in order to learn something about them and from them" (Moschella, 2008, p. 4). Naturally, this requires a humble posture as we encounter those who are culturally different from ourselves.

Background Research

For many, the first step in researching a new culture is to start reading a book or articles about that culture. That is actually a good start that can provide a general working knowledge of the culture we are encountering. Gaining some background information concerning the history and country of origin of a particular community will provide a helpful starting point for our learning. However, it is important to remember that once people begin immigrating to a new society, they experience degrees of change and cultural adaptation. We should expect some aspects of an ethnic enclave to reflect the basic cultural information that we have learned, while at the same time, we will discover unique adaptations and cultural hybrids emerging due to the experience of immigration. Often, members of ethnic enclaves in our city will reflect a blend of their home culture and their new host culture. Nevertheless, background reading is certainly helpful as long as we approach the cultural group as someone who is prepared to learn new insights and face new challenges.

We might find two kinds of background reading particularly helpful for reaching out cross-culturally in the diverse and constantly changing environment of globalization. First, it will be helpful to do background research on the culture of the city. The city will often integrate new immigrants into its neighborhoods and change their lives as much as they also impact the cultural fabric of the city. Large and famous cities, such as New York City or San Francisco, may have a greater resource of sociological and historical work available, but most cities will have at least some resources for learning about the history and culture of the city itself. Gaining a greater understanding of the environment of the host city potentially may offer insight into how the new setting may impact newcomers from different nations. This will be especially important for new church planters or ministers still learning about their ministry context.

Secondly, one may find books and articles that describe particular ethnic groups. Historical or anthropological texts may provide helpful insights into the background of a particular people. If a ministry is attempting to reach a certain diaspora community in their city or region, it is helpful to learn at least a rudimentary knowledge about their country of origin. By learning about the background of a people and by learning about the nature of the city where they have become established as a community, the Christian worker may begin to gain a general understanding of the diaspora community within her ministry context. This is not a definitive grasp on the culture and journey of migration of the community. There is still much to learn, but this can be a good start.

Taking Notes

Most of the activities you will need to pursue will involve hands-on learning incorporating intentional observation and learning to ask good questions. It may seem trivial to say, but it will be important to take notes. Often it will not be possible to take notes in the middle of conversations or during participation in cultural activities, but as soon as you step away and have the opportunity, you will want to take down some notes that help you capture the memory of what you just experienced. An important research practice for learning and processing our cross-cultural experiences is to write down the descriptions of our experiences on the same day. It may be better to jot down many brief notes than to attempt to recall everything in one long log. The point is, we want to describe what we have experienced while the memory is recent and unclouded by further analysis. We want to be able to go back to our notes later and trust that they captured the experience, as close to the moment as possible (Bernard, 2006, pp. 387–389).

In New York City, our outreach teams realized early on they could take notes about cultural learning experiences on a smartphone without anyone in the community realizing what they were doing. Rather than looking like scientists with clipboards, our team members may have appeared to be updating Facebook statuses, sending e-mails, or jotting down to-do lists rather than taking field notes. Some teams have also created a private Google document where team members could all share a common set of field notes and learning experiences in order to build their understanding, as a team, of the cultural group with whom they are working. Storing the document in the cloud, everyone on the team has access to it, so every team member shares in collaborative cultural learning as every member of the team adds notes from their encounters in the community.

On some occasions, it is appropriate to take notes visibly in front of your friend. I (Seth) remember speaking to a Bengali man about how to raise children well. I asked him what was important for Bengali parents to teach their children to help them grow to mature adults—a helpful ethnographic question, but also a normal inquiry in conversation. When he began to speak, I said, "What you say seems really wise. Is it alright if I write this down?" He was pleased that I would want to remember it and felt respected that I would ask.

When taking notes, remember to write down descriptions. Begin by just describing what you are seeing, hearing, and experiencing. Avoid jumping too quickly to analyzing your experiences, as you might miss something important or allow your assumptions to cloud your judgment. Instead, describe what you see and hear and then go back and assess what you have experienced later when you can step back and take everything into account beyond a single instance.

Participant Observation

One of the key practices for learning to listen well to the cultures we intend to engage is the act of the participant observation. In participant observation, we step into the midst of culture as learners in order to discover bridges for the Gospel between ourselves as messengers and members of a specific community. We seek avenues for sharing activities and experiences with our diaspora neighbors as intentionally attentive participants desiring to learn from our observations and experiences. "Participant observation involves going out and staying out, and learning a new language (or a new dialect of a language you already know), and experiencing the lives of the people you are studying as much as you can" (Bernard, 2006, p. 344). Participant observation is the practice of stepping into the middle of a cultural scene and watching, listening, and learning everything we possibly can. We learn through observing and experiencing the culture in action.

As we begin interacting with a new culture, we want to do more than watch from a distance. Rather, a good researcher will find opportunities for taking notes and reflecting on what can be learned. Notes should be made describing observations with significant detail in order to analyze the conversations, relationships, events, non-verbals, and what they might mean (Wan & Casey, 2014). Participant observation is more than just people-watching. It is not mere passive observation but is a practice of crossing cultures to interact with people in their own cultural context and learning as much as possible from the experience. In order to learn proactively through various cross-cultural experiences, we should seek to build "explicit awareness." In other words, we must strive to gain awareness of the little details during cultural exchanges in order to build our insights into the ethnic community with whom we are interacting (Bernard, 2006, pp. 364-365). Learning all we can about a culture is an act of love. We refrain from assuming our way is best but rather seeking understanding so that we can show respect and communicate love among those who are culturally different from ourselves. We hope to communicate with them respectfully and communicate good news in a way that they can grasp and make their own. While it will be impossible for us to know a culture the same way as an insider to the culture, we want to be able to transmit the Gospel in a way that makes sense to the hearer.

When we enter into an ethnic network or neighborhood, we will have different opportunities to learn, listen, and observe. In the beginning, we may be limited by how much access we have been given. If we have a ministry partner, cultural informant, or gatekeeper from the actual community that we are learning about, we may consider going with them the first time or two that we explore the neighborhood. In a later chapter we will discuss how to go about identifying and forming relationships with gatekeepers and cultural informants, but for now it is important to note that entering the community with a cultural insider may enhance our experience by helping us to see things that we otherwise would miss or take a rather long time to recognize (Wan & Casey, 2014, p. 70).

When we enter a community as a participant observer, we must begin to build some specific skills to help us learn all we can about the culture we are encountering. Evangelists entering a new cultural world should begin to build "explicit awareness" of the many details occurring all around them, and many of us do not automatically recall what we see and hear later on when it is time to write our notes for the day. Therefore, another key skill is improving our memory. Sometimes, when you have had a meaningful interaction or set of observations, it is best not to speak with anyone or pursue additional interactions until you can take some notes. As learners, we should take advantage of our ignorance of the culture and seek to learn everything we can. In our humility, we have the opportunity to become a student and soak up as much information as possible. Of course, there are times when our expertise in something is our ticket of acceptance into the community, so while we are entering as learners, at the same time we would not want to leave an impression of ignorance or social incompetence.

Repetition, too, is an important aspect of observation. We never want to draw formal conclusions from a single observation of an event or behavior. Many times we may hear a person speak with a particular phrasing or see a specific interaction and feel tempted to rush from observation to conclusion; this is an ethnographic error to which those first practicing cross-cultural ministry are especially vulnerable. It is easy to observe something once in a single instance and jump to an inaccurate conclusion. We could make any number of observations that don't necessarily mean what we think they mean at first impression:

- o "She calls the god Krishna but then he says 'Lord Krishna' so that must mean...."
- o "She used far more hand gestures when speaking to her uncle than her father, so I should too...."
- o "There are a disproportionate number of people wearing yellow today, and it is a Thursday; this must be significant...."
- o "The imam dyes his beard orange so I should expect anyone with an orange beard to be an imam...."

When you first begin to learn about and observe a community, it is best to wait until you have seen an action performed multiple times by different people in the community before trying to draw conclusions about its significance or meaning. Imagine meeting an American who does not eat beef and concluding that all Americans do not eat beef. It could have been true—like Jewish and Muslim attitudes towards pork—but it would be unwise to draw a universal conclusion about a culture or subculture from a single conversation.

As we learn about a culture, it is important that we practice a degree of objectivity. While no human being can be completely objective, we can be aware of our own thoughts, ideas, and biases. Quite often individuals fall into the trap of failing "to suspend judgment about differences in behavior because they assume unconsciously that their own ways are normal, natural, and right" (Stewart & Bennett, 1991, p. 3). This is not to say that we should not hold onto beliefs and activities that are rooted in Scripture and reflect Christ-like behavior, but when we grow in our cultural sensitivity, we often begin to recognize how many of our assumptions are cultural, rather than purely biblical. This too, is a skill individuals will need to build in order to carry the Gospel cross-culturally. Ultimately, we must learn to be ourselves (others know when we are faking it) while being culturally sensitive and attentive as learners. Frankly, "it may sound silly, but just hanging out is a skill, and until you learn it you cannot do your best work as a participant observer" (Bernard, 2006, pp. 364–372).

Levels of Participant Observation

There are different levels of participant observation. The three most basic levels are: non-participation, partial participation, and full participation (Wan & Casey, 2014, p. 71). In non-participation we are physically present in a community but keeping our distance. Non-participation can be a great starting point, but if we only practice non-participation, we will severely limit our learning opportunities. This passive approach to participation might make sense on our first walk through a neighborhood, in order to get a sense of the flow of cultures and interactions going on around us. We might find a market or coffee shop where we can sit and observe what is going on, who is doing business there, who lives there, who shops there, etc. Often, I (Jared) will enter a store or restaurant and immediately try to observe everything I can see around me. I want to find out everything I can from the social interactions, products in the store, and other details. When I enter a Mexican cafe, I can observe several artworks that represent the culture, or when I am in a grocery store in an Arab neighborhood, I might recognize the nations they are serving by observing the countries and languages associated with various products. As I walk past a Bengali grocery store used for a Muslim prayer time for a group of men in the community, I can casually look in and see how they structure their worship in a limited semi-public space. We can learn a great deal with our eyes wide open to all of our surroundings.

Partial participation takes place when we are able to join in activities. We are not a key player in the particular activity, but we have begun to build relationships and start conversations. We are able to ask questions and start to get a sense of the different activities that are meaningful to a group of people. Partial participation will likely be a meaningful form of interaction for Christian evangelists in an ethnic community or network. It will be an opportunity to be a humble learner since we will often be experiencing a new activity—or perhaps a different approach to a familiar activity. I (Seth) remember attending the baby shower of Jamaican friends. The party had a dance floor, a three-course meal, and a professional DJ. I had no role in the ceremonies, so I was able to ask questions of fellow guests like: "Was this similar to your baby shower? Are these the same guests who came to the wedding? Do most parties have this same kind of food?" This level of participation allows us to begin entering the community, but we should not expect to be fully integrated during these early encounters.

Full participation occurs when we enter into a more central role in a new cultural activity. When a pastor in the church is asked by a Mexican family to play a key role in their daughter's *quinceañera*, he is playing an important part in that community, but it is also an opportunity to learn through a deeper level of experience from an inside view.

Similarly, some years ago when I (Jared) was asked to bless a newborn baby by a non-religious Latino family, I accepted. Due to my own theological position, I explained that I did not baptize infants, but I would gladly facilitate a time of prayer and blessing. They were eager to have me conduct a blessing and prayer service in their home. When I arrived, I found many of the elements that would be present in a traditional ceremony despite their significant distance from any previous religious practice as a family. The small child was in a white dress, godparents were present, and a huge meal was prepared in celebration. Despite the theological shift that I brought to the experience and the families relative lack of religious experience themselves, the family contextualized this event in cultural terms that were meaningful to them based on a cultural heritage that still resonated with them despite their own lack of personal religious experience. Even though the ceremony was a cultural hybrid, it was an opportunity to observe what elements were most important for the family to preserve from within their ethnic community's religious traditions even though they themselves had mostly been outside of any meaningful church involvement for multiple generations of their family.

Asking Ethnographic Questions

If we want to learn about a culture, we must learn to ask perceptive questions. While we will never be totally inside of their culture, becoming a learner demonstrates both our respect for them as a people and our desire for the Gospel to deeply impact every nation. The higher degree to which we can learn about their cultural world, the more we can communicate good news in a way that makes sense to them, and the more effectively we can coach new believers to embody a Gospel presence among the members of their own cultural group and ethnic community. It is the members of the community themselves who will contextualize the message of good news for their own cultural community, but an important role of the cross-cultural evangelist is to become a theologically-rooted and culturally sensitive coach to help guide the process.

One of the primary research tools is asking ethnographic questions. "Here the researcher asks a limited number of questions and encourages the interviewee to provide details and depth on their experiences. In this way, the researcher can let the research build a theory about what is going on in the area and not import foreign explanations" (Wan & Casey, 2014, p. 72). Asking appropriate questions is one of the most important skills to develop as a cross-cultural worker.

There are different approaches to ethnographic interviewing. Cross-cultural evangelists often make use of informal interviewing. This approach to asking questions is often appropriate in ministry settings because it takes the shape of everyday conversations. Those at the other end do not always realize that you are thinking of it as ethnographic research because you are asking important questions in the context of regular conversations. (Bernard, 2006, pp. 210–211). You can actually learn a great deal by asking about daily life for the members of a specific cultural group, stepping away and taking good notes, and later reviewing what you have learned from the day's interactions. Through simple questions, you can begin to learn key bits of information with each adding a different piece to the puzzle.

When asking questions, it is important to keep in mind the difference between the information you are seeking and what is conversationally appropriate. You might want to know of your community: "What time of day are people most available for hanging out? Who are the important and influential people in the community? How do people here tend to feel about different types of outsiders coming into their neighborhood? What are the general attitudes towards religion?" You will need to ask questions naturally, however, in a way that is informal and conversational. For example, you might consider rephrasing the questions above, like so: "I am surprised to see your store open this late. Do you always work this time of day? When do you take time to relax? I was thinking about having a barbecue in the neighborhood, who would be good to advise me on the best way to plan that? I noticed many of your signs are in Korean. Do most of your customers read Korean?" For a number of ethnographic sample questions, see the appendices at the end of this book.

Of course, as you continue digging, you want to discover insights that will greatly affect your work as an evangelist. For instance, how are major life decisions made: through group consensus, under the influence of a family patriarch, entirely as individuals, or some other way? How much has the experience of immigration begun to fragment and change this community? To what degree do they reflect their country of origin in customs and traditions? One of the main challenges of more informal approaches to ethnographic inquiry is to remember that you are seeking information. It is easy to get lost in the enjoyment of conversations with your friends and forget that you are trying to build a picture of the cultural group you are hoping to reach. A key motive for gathering information about the culture is to communicate love effectively. We want to communicate the truth and hope of the Gospel, and to embody the love of Jesus respectfully in our interactions. In addition, while we will certainly make mistakes, we want to avoid unnecessary errors that could have been avoided by some basic cultural research.

Other types of ethnographic questioning include: unstructured interviewing, semi-structured interviewing, or structured interviewing. In unstructured interviewing, both the researcher and the interviewee know they are being interviewed. This approach is more than simply inserting questions into a conversation. The interviewer has a plan and asks questions, but she exercises little or no control over the responses. The person being interviewed is given the space to open up and express their thoughts freely. Semi-structured interviewing is similar to unstructured interviewing in that the one responding to the questions has maximum latitude to respond as they wish; the difference being that the interviewer uses a pre-determined set of questions and topics with a plan to move through them in a certain order. Finally, in structured interviews, "people are asked to respond to as nearly identical a set of stimuli as possible," and interviewers are working with a strict set of parameters for the interview (Bernard, 2006, pp. 211–212). Most often, a cross-cultural evangelist in an immigrant community will ask ethnographic questions in the context of either informal or unstructured approaches, but there may be ministry settings where a church has access to a specific community through a formal outreach program and semi-structured or structured interviews are both possible and appropriate.

Most church leaders do not have time to commit to a long regimen of studying interview methods. There simply is not enough time, and the opportunities and challenges facing their church are urgent. Yet there are some basic skills one can grasp quickly and begin learning while on the job. We believe that most church leaders possess the humility and the relational skill sets to take some of the basic principles and keep learning as they go. We want to encourage you to enter a community and start learning all that you can. You will not be an expert at the beginning, but with the mindset of a learner, you will rapidly grow in your basic understanding of the community and present a profound testimony through your humility. Many immigrants have few experiences of Americans from the dominant culture seeking to learn from *them* as immigrants, practice *their* language, and thoughtfully consider *their* perspective. Doing so is a ministry to our newest neighbors originating from other nations. The best teacher is experience, but there are a few basics that can help you learn as much as possible from your experience in a new community.

First, remember to listen. Listen to what is said, and be alert to what is not said. Second, be attentive to everything happening around you. As cultural outsiders we may miss subtle cues. Sometimes we observe something that is not actually very important, but when we start to see a pattern emerge after several visits in the community, we begin to be able to assign meaning to the activities that we are observing. Third, ask open-ended questions. If you have done pastoral counseling, think about the types of questions that are most helpful in counseling sessions? Which is more productive, to ask, "Do you love your father?" or "Tell me about your father." The former question requires only a "yes/no" answer, whereas the latter question opens the door to deeper insights. Learning cultural information is much the same way. Yes/no or one-word-answer questions will get us exactly what we have asked for, but open-ended questions have the potential to get willing informants talking and provide you with a treasure chest of information about the local community. Remember to avoid asking "why?" questions. Asking "why?" pushes others to analyze their motives and risks suggesting that you are judging their responses (McCurdy et al., 2004, p. 38). Fourth, never pretend to know more than you do or assume that your knowledge is complete. It is always appropriate to say, "I don't know much about that, could you tell me more?" Our willingness to listen and learn is what will ultimately create the trust necessary for our friends to reciprocate as we begin sharing the message of Jesus.

Do not get ahead of yourself and rush to analysis. Get rich descriptions from members of the diaspora community in their own words. Allow the descriptions to flow from their experiences, and try to remember to record notes as close to their words as possible. Later, when you have notes from a variety of people that you have listened to, you will be able to begin analysis of your experiences. Jumping into analysis too quickly runs the danger of inserting our own assumptions into the process and derailing the most insightful lessons.

In addition, it is a good idea to engage multiple people in the community with your questions. Find different people in different social settings as well as of a variety of ages. Try to discover who the gatekeepers are in that community and those who can speak accurately about the culture. When you find someone who is helpful to you, attempt to have them connect you to others who might be equally as helpful (Wan & Casey, 2014, p. 73).

When learning about another culture, it is important that we suspend judgment. It is a temptation to pounce on ideas that we feel are theologically "off." That is certainly my (Jared's) instinct. However, by doing so we may short circuit the whole process that is intended to lead to a healthy theological orientation. At the same time, we should not be shy about asking questions. We will make mistakes, and a paralyzing fear of failure virtually guarantees the sort of failure we wish to avoid. We need to take the leap; just do so with humility.

Types of Questions

James Spradley gives us three basic types of questions for gathering cultural information that any Christian leader can learn to ask: descriptive questions, structural questions, and contrast questions. Descriptive questions do just that: they ask for descriptions. They encourage someone to tell the story of their own people in their own words. Structural questions attempt to discover what sorts of categories exist and how different things are classified within a cultural group. Contrast questions search out how people distinguish differences. You might ask, "What is the difference between..." in order to explore how they differentiate between aspects of everyday life (Spradley, 1979, pp. 78–184).

In the context of diaspora communities, learning to ask these types of questions can help the minister get to know a nearby cultural community at a much deeper level in order to serve the community more effectively. For example, you might ask an international friend about the differences between life in their country of origin and life in their new community in an American city. As they explain the contrast between these two places in their personal story, you may begin learning how their life has changed to adapt to a new place as well as what traditional cultural elements they have maintained in their new environment. Such a question would likely open up the opportunity for several follow-up questions as well.

Here is one example of a sequence of questioning that dives into a greater understanding of a religious practice. For this example, stepping into one side of the conversation we will use something familiar to many Christian readers.

- *What are churches in your denomination like?*
- *That is interesting. What kinds of things happen in a typical worship service?*
- *Oh, so the altar call sounds important. What is the significance of an altar call?*
- *What takes place during an altar call?*
- *Can you remember ever participating in an altar call yourself? What happened?*

You can see the sequence of these questions. They begin with a broad question to guide the conversation into some initial descriptions. While answering the first question, the respondent will likely mention a number of different topics, but rather than attempt to chase all of them, the researcher focuses in on one aspect of the religious culture—the worship service—in order to learn deeply about that aspect of their religious life. Listening to the description of the worship service, the "altar call" catches the researcher's attention, so she asks about that ritual and seeks more a detailed description. Finally, if it has not already come up, the researcher attempts to discover if there are any personal examples in the history of her conversation partner. This last question shifts the descriptions from something like a third party event to explore emotional connections, personal significance, the impact on one's spirituality, and similar discoveries.

When asking open-ended questions, you are attempting to draw out descriptive answers from your conversation partners in order to learn all you can about their perspective of life within their cultural and religious experiences. Learning to probe is an essential skill to fruitful ethnographic learning. Your conversation partner may give you a good bit of information, but in an attempt to see if there is more, you may simply offer an "uh-huh," or you may wait several seconds in silence during a pause while they collect their thoughts instead of jumping in and cutting their explanation short. Another way to probe may be to simply say something like, "That is interesting. Tell me more about that." There are a number of ways to probe in an information-gathering conversation, but the key is to make sure you are getting all the information you can from your conversation partner. You do not want to jump in and cut their descriptions short. Rather you want to nudge them to keep talking, so you have the opportunity to learn all that you possibly can (Bernard, 2006, pp. 217–223).

As you begin to evaluate what you are experiencing through observation and asking ethnographic questions, a key discipline is to guard against any underlying feelings of superiority. We might not even be conscious of assumptions lying under the surface. We are all vulnerable to interpreting different cultures with an ethnocentric perspective. As we examine the evidence, the cross-cultural worker may come to realize where she has previously judged incorrectly or imposed pre-existing biases upon those who are culturally different (Ortiz & Conn, 2001, p. 285). Suspending judgment as a researcher and remaining aware of our own cultural presuppositions as we enter into evangelistic relationships are two important principles to remember when, as cross-cultural ministers, we attempt to facilitate the Gospel taking root in international communities. This is reinforced when approaching diaspora networks because change is a constant in these communities. It is important to recognize how much we don't know and discipline our tendency to make assumptions as we cross cultures into a new community that is likely to be experiencing challenges and changes that we may not fully understand.

Practice

1. Identify a culturally distinct neighborhood in your area and find a business or public space to travel to within it. Start out by practicing passive observation. Find a spot where you can easily observe interactions. It may be a park, sporting event, food court, or other public area. As soon as you leave, take some notes about what you observed. Don't jump to conclusions; stick to writing descriptions.

2. Practice asking open-ended questions. Go to a culturally specific market or cafe. Attempt to strike up conversations and intentionally stick to using open-ended questions. If they begin describing something from their culture, try subtly probing in order to encourage a more thorough description. Again, as soon as you leave, take some notes about what you observed and what you heard in conversation. Do not jump to conclusions; stick to writing descriptions.

Chapter 3

The Gospel Enters our World

The task of culture is to take all of the aspects and elements experienced within a group and to integrate them into a shared framework. This is not to suggest that any culture has a singular perspective on a given issue, but rather, that cultures tend to build foundational myths that its members appeal to and use in various ways to account for the community's experiences. Diverse beliefs, values, and behaviors exist in the broader culture, but these tend to stem from different interpretations and implementations of the same myths. Let us suggest two primary ways to think about culture (Deleuze & Guattari, 1987). The first is a foundational understanding of culture. This seems to be the popular way that we often understand cultural identities. For instance, we might believe that we are first Americans and that other cultural identities are subservient to this dominant identity. In this model, the dominant culture is the foundational layer and the community filters down to smaller, more specific subcultures. Think of the foundational model of culture like an upside down pyramid, with each subculture narrowing down from the one above it. Using as an example my (Seth's) hometown of Amarillo, TX, a graphic depiction might look something like this:

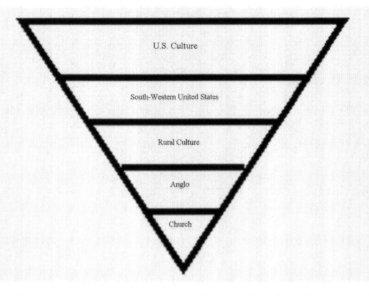

Each of these is a true facet of an individual's cultural orientation, and we can see how the foundational model helps us understand the cultural layers in which such a person might be involved. If the individual in question were from an urban rather than a more rural culture, or a Latino rather than from an Anglo-American community, he would still be engaged with many of the same levels of culture, but there would be some significant changes in myths or cultural identities which would need to be accounted for. Migrating from one's own culture of origin to a foreign society is often disorienting and triggers a destabilization in cultural foundations. In a foundational model, it is important to raise questions about what happens when the higher tiers of culture begin to shift, as they do for our diaspora neighbors. How do our immigrant friends begin to reform their foundational cultural myths when the foundation itself has been shattered? Such questions expose the limitations of the foundational model. This model is helpful for understanding communities or individuals with a stable cultural location, but it does little to help us understand cultural identities in transition.

As an alternative to the foundational model, we might understand culture through a networked model. Rather than a pyramid, we might envision this model as a spider web. Unlike the foundational model, where each level of the pyramid contained a separate and, to an extent, self-contained compartment of cultural identity, in the networked model, one's identity is invested in the structure as a whole. The structure is grounded by its attachment to multiple identities, each cultural thread bringing with it its own myths (Bouchelle, January 28, 2013). Taking my Puerto Rican friend Ray from the Bronx as an example, we might picture his identity in the networked model like this:

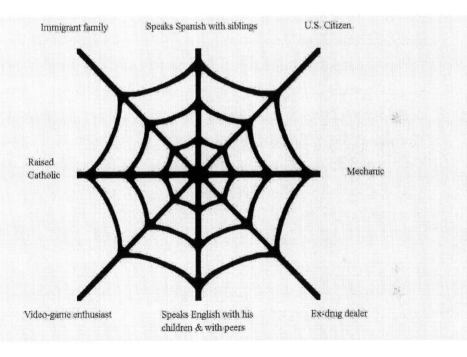

Immigrant family   Speaks Spanish with siblings   U.S. Citizen

Raised Catholic   Mechanic

Video-game enthusiast   Speaks English with his children & with peers   Ex-drug dealer

As you can see, one advantage of the networked model is that it allows us to understand cultural identity when a community or individual holds multiple identities that are interacting and sometimes in conflict with one another. In global societies, "identities are never either pure or fixed but formed at the intersections of age, class, gender, race and nation" (Barker, 2003, p. 260). Ray functions in separate worlds on a regular basis. He has identity formed with the flexibility to move between cultural worlds. On one hand, he is a U.S. citizen because he was born in a U.S. territory, and he has spent most of his life in New York City. When I (Seth) spend an evening in his home, there is little sense of crossing cultures. However, Ray also enters seamlessly into certain groups of Latino immigrants. Because of the general perception of Puerto Ricans as culturally distinct by many non-Latinos in the U.S., he understands what it means to be seen as an immigrant and "non-American" in a way his children never will. However, his networked identity in regards to nation of origin does not extend to many other people groups in the city. Growing up as a native of the Bronx, Ray has little love for the Muslim diaspora moving in and, as he sees it, "taking over his neighborhood." Because of his past gang involvement, some of his social contacts bring flashes of drama and violence into his life, conflicting with his otherwise quite stable, middle-class profile.

Ray represents what has come to be the new normal in the urban world: a cultural identity grounded in multiple seemingly incompatible worlds, worlds which would make it all but impossible to integrate his myths into the hierarchical structure of the foundational model of culture. In a multicultural society, individuals may have "shifting identifications" as well as "hybrid identities" drawing on multiple cultural sources (Barker, 2003, p. 260). Therefore, realizing one's cultural identity in a global context may involve recognizing the web of cultural influences and experiences that make up the urban person. In a multicultural city, identifying a person's identity based on a cultural generalization may not tell the whole story.

Once we begin to understand the web of an individual's or community's cultural identity, in order to speak the Gospel adequately to that culture, we must begin to understand the many facets in which given myths are already operating within that culture and whether these narratives are compatible with the Gospel, bridges to the Gospel, or are in opposition to the message we bring. For example, many of my (Seth's) Bengali friends have come to New York City to make money to support extended families still overseas. The US Bengali diaspora sent $694 million in remittances to Bangladesh in 2012 alone (*The Bangladeshi Diaspora in the United States* July 2014), and global remittances are one of the foundational motivations behind international migration. For Bengalis, this is a sacrificial service by which they can provide stability for their community back home. This experience is a great bridge to share a story like one of *Isa*'s (Jesus') parables and communicate that they may be in an advantageous position to begin to understand the teachings in the *Injil (Gospel)*. For others, however, this lifestyle has caused financial security to take the highest importance in their lives, and they now see their position as a way to advance in caste, making social status more primary than even religious devotion. We need to listen well in order to discover the points of compatibility or conflict with the Gospel. (D. Garrison, personal communication, 2015).

Mosaic

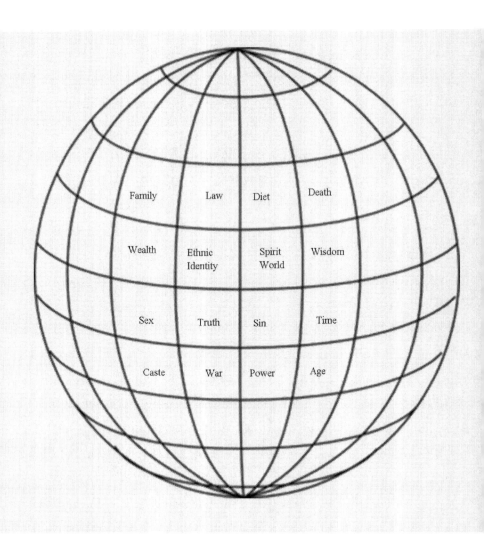

Practice One

Identifying Culture

This is a first step in contextualization: identifying the aspects most influenced by culture and understanding their relationship to the Gospel. After determining the primary culture you plan to minister to, in the following spaces, identify your initial impressions of the culture. This will provide a guide for the remainder of the study. What is the cultural orientation towards:

Time-

Caste/Social Class-

Wisdom/Truth-

Authority-

As you have interacted with people from the cultural group you hope to reach, what are some other key areas of cultural concern you have observed? Based on your observation, list other concepts important to your diaspora neighbor's culture:

Concerning the following statements, mark the one answer that best describes your own culture, then mark the answer that best fits the identified people group to which you plan to minister:

Group identity is based on:

☐ *nation/citizenship* ☐ *region* ☐ *tribe/race*

☐ *language* ☐*religion*

Wrong doing describes an act against:

☐ *the law* ☐ *the community* ☐ *the spiritual order*

Major community decisions are made by:

☐ *the legislature* ☐ *the elders* ☐*the shaman/priest*

Major holidays are linked to:

☐ *nation's history* ☐ *religious events* ☐ *the seasonal cycle*

Social leaders usually consult:

☐ *scientific experts* ☐ *tradition* ☐ *spiritual authorities*

Regarding social status within the culture that you are encountering, rank the following from highest to lowest status (1-8):

____ Children ____ Mothers

____ Young Men ____ Grandparents

____ Young Women ____ Extended Relatives

____ Fathers ____ Unrelated Elders

Regarding the culture, rank the following from most important to least (1-7):

____ Work

____ Family

____ Communal events

____ Religious observation

____ Rest

____ Recreation

____ Gender specific activities

As you review the information you have just outlined, reflect on whether or not the Gospels speak to any of these topics and, if so, in what way. In the New Testament, how do we see communities interacting with the various aspects of culture? For instance, what cultural narratives can you see playing within the epistles? How did the Gospel challenge or affirm these communities?

Questions for further reflection

1. What are ways that your own culture corresponds or relates to your diaspora neighbor's culture?

2. Where are the most significant differences between your culture and your neighbor's culture?

3. Can you state in your own words any of the myths that might underlie these beliefs or values?

4. Is this an area where the Gospel affirms, challenges, or is it neutral?

Practice Two

Forming Narratives

As we have stated, although various communities in a culture may share common myths, the working out of those myths can differ greatly across various groups. This can be the result of two distinct activities that we are often not attentive to: the prioritizing of certain myths as central or peripheral and the developing of myths into different narratives. Narratives represent the working out of myths into larger, more directed structures and stories. The subtle differences in adapting myth into narrative account for many differences within culture.

To understand narrative, we would suggest using the following questions as a template (Sheldrake, 2007, p. 34):

1. What is the purpose or need that must be realized?
2. What are the obstacles to that taking place?
3. Where does this take place?
4. What are the means by which it takes place?
5. What does the final product look like?

So let us compare possible narratives around death that might emerge from the interaction between an American worker and her Hindu diaspora neighbor. (a) In forming a narrative around the understanding and engagement with death, an American worker might see the purpose or intended realization of her actions to be the memorialization of the deceased as an expression of grief and respect. (b) An obstacle to this honorary remembrance may be the lack of familial proximity. (c) A formal gathering, then, accomplishes the task of memorialization, (d) as it gathers together the family and friends and allows them to share stories which honor the deceased in preparation for their burial. (e) The final result is a funeral service.

In contrast, (a) our Hindu neighbor may see the primary purpose of their engagement with death as the preparation of the deceased's soul for reincarnation and petition to the gods on behalf of the loved one. (b) The obstacles to this taking place may be an ignorance of proper ritual on the part of the family. (c) The proper procedures, then, would need to take place in proximity to the appropriate religious experts and spiritual setting (d) and they would be accomplished when the rituals were faithfully carried out. (e) The final result would be that the soul of the deceased successfully transitions to its next place in the cycle of life and death.

Now practice constructing a few narratives of your own. For example, let us take two institutions which all cultures share: marriage (what is the purpose or ideal) and social value of age (is youth or age more valued?). In the following space, state the involved myths and using the five questions just listed above, diagram the way in which your own culture and that of your diaspora neighbor's culture integrate these myths into narrative:

Aging

Your Culture	Neighbor's Culture
The myth:	
1.	
2.	
3.	
4.	
5.	

Marriage

Your Culture	Neighbor's Culture
The myth:	
1.	
2.	
3.	
4.	
5.	

As we start to understand the way that narratives work in relation to myth, we need to assess the cross-cultural communication that we might construct based on the Gospels. It is important to remember that even when we believe an element of our culture is "biblically based," we still live in a different culture than the writers of Scripture, and the same principle or truth may look radically different when faithfully applied in the culture of our diaspora neighbors. To go a step further, it can be helpful to keep in mind that in regards to family, hospitality, taboo, the spiritual world, and many other myths, the cultures of the majority world are often much closer to the cultural world from which our Scriptures emerged than our North American cultures. They may, in fact, have a better intuitive grasp of many issues we see in Scripture than we ourselves might possess. Indeed, there is much to learn through discussions with our diaspora neighbors from around the world.

Practice Three

Case Study

Your friend Salam is a new immigrant from Bangladesh. He works at the local Subway restaurant and out of his wages supports not only himself and his mother, but also the families of two of his brothers and his sister. You are helping him practice his English so that he may find more gainful employment. Salam is worried that he is no longer a good Muslim because in order to make ends meet he must work 60–70 hours a week, preventing him from attending *masjid* (mosque) to do his prayers and often from participating in religious festivals like *Eid*. Although he still tries to eat *halal* foods (Islamic diet) and refrains from drinking alcohol, he feels shame when he talks about religion because from his perspective he knows that he has not followed the law adequately to please *Allah*.

Using the information from this chapter, identify any myths or narratives you feel are relevant to understanding Salam's situation, then select a story or parable from the Gospel which you might be able to share with Salam which would correspond to his situation. How can you proclaim good news to him? As you select something from a biblical perspective to share, remember to think through how the content will need to be contextualized in order for him to understand the points you are making.

Notes:

Chapter 4

Discerning Your Ministry Approach

We expect the readers of this book represent a variety of ministry contexts throughout North America. Some may be leaders of growing multiethnic churches who want to become even more effective at reaching out into the diversity of their surrounding community. Others are part of churches that have experienced a change in their neighborhood demographics and are struggling to discern how to engage cultural groups with whom they have, as of yet, little real experience. Still others might be church planters hoping to enter a community in a metro area and realizing that crossing cultures will be an important component of their new ministry. Finally, we expect some will be students of cross-cultural ministry seeking to apply what they are presently learning to a society deeply impacted by globalization.

Regardless of your situation, once you begin diving into a community and truly learning from the cultural groups located there, what do you do next? You have asked questions, observed community activities, collected pages of notes based on your experiences, and spent time with families in homes and community activities. How will everything you have learned affect how you and your church pursue the next steps of ministry among your newest neighbors? We do not intend to offer an exact answer to that question. The potential answers for each ministry scenario are as specific and as unique as the ministry contexts and individual neighborhoods themselves. However, we do want to spark strategic thinking and offer foundations for discernment as you face the ministry choices emerging from your cultural exploration. In this chapter we would like to offer some guidance for determining your church's strategies for reaching an ethnic community or network located in your city.

One of the foundational assumptions of this chapter is that we, as Christians, are motivated to participate in the growth of God's Kingdom even beyond our individual organizational expressions of God's mission. This assumption has implications for how we discuss ministry and outreach strategies in this book. Both authors work through Global City Mission Initiative. We believe in its purpose, and therefore, we work towards its increasing maturity and actual growth as a Christian ministry. Nevertheless, our primary driving motivation should be our participation in the continuing expansion of God's Kingdom first; and the growth of our own organizational expression of that mission should always be superseded by the larger concern for God's global mission.

While our own ministry efforts certainly represent wonderful expressions of God's work through His people, as Christians our deepest motivations should align our efforts with God's mission in His world. We must, therefore, ask ourselves the question: Is our primary purpose to increase our church's membership roll, or is it to expand the reach of God's Kingdom in our city? Naturally, we want to see our church's membership grow, and growing your individual congregation's attendance is not a goal in opposition to Kingdom centered ministry. That passion for growth may be a good and healthy desire. However, our primary purpose for engaging our neighborhoods with the Gospel is to help facilitate the expansion of God's reign among every people, tribe, and nation. We certainly can have both, but we believe we need to discipline our ministry strategies in such a way that prioritizes our primary purpose for ministry.

This outward focus also propels us as witnesses of the Gospel beyond the comfortable boundaries of the Christian church and into cultures and communities of families and peoples that have yet to bow their knee to Jesus as Lord. It may cause us to pursue quality ministry that is difficult to measure or report rapidly. This prioritization may lead us to empower others from the community to lead and to take credit for things in which we have invested ourselves deeply. A Kingdom-centered mission strategy may produce a multitude of fruit and impact our church community in amazing ways, but at times it may make little or no visible changes to the everyday work taking place inside our church buildings. Aligning ourselves with God's bigger picture helps us navigate faithfully the road ahead when engaging culturally different communities.

Types of Ethnic Communities

It is important to recognize that there is a great deal of diversity among immigrant communities. Most immigrants live between worlds. They are learning to cope with the new world of the dominant culture while simultaneously maintaining ties with their countries of origin. This being the case, ethnic communities often represent a spectrum of assimilation with individuals, families, neighborhoods, and ethnic networks existing across a broad continuum (Looney, 2015, pp. 187–

192). Stepping into neighborhoods and networks of new international migrants, Enoch Wan and Anthony Casey have framed patterns of cultural assimilation among ethnic immigrant groups into three different profiles.

"The first assimilation pattern is the *ethnic enclave* where immigrants of the same or similar cultural backgrounds group into a geographically dense section of the city and rely on an ethnically driven local economy." This provides a space to escape the pressures of assimilation and where members of the community can freely speak their first language. (Wan & Casey, 2014, p. 107). Neighborhoods like Manhattan's Little Senegal, Nashville's Little Kurdistan, or Houston's Northside represent just a few examples of the numerous ethnic enclaves dotting the landscape of our cities. Whether Cuban, Irish, Chinese, or North African, clusters of immigrants from various parts of the world frequently form geographically distinct communities that provide an economic niche and preserve ethnic identities. Within these urban spaces, they carve out a home away from home.

"A second pattern of assimilation is the *cultural threads* model where immigrants of the same ethnic group do not live in close geographic proximity but are closely linked through a variety of social networks." In this case, people sharing a common ethnic identity do not necessarily live in close proximity, but they maintain tight connections. Virtual communities through online social media, business associations, ethnic markets, restaurants, religious assemblies, and other points of common connection keep people with a shared ethnic identity connected through networks despite a lack of neighborhood proximity (Wan & Casey, 2014, pp. 107–108). Sometimes these networks remain unnoticed by Christian leaders in a city because there is not a specific ethnic enclave to point to; however, ethnic networks in a metro region can be quite expansive.

Wan and Casey describe a third pattern of ethnic assimilation, the *urban tribe* model, in which different ethnic groups create a multi-ethnic community built on common affinities rather than primarily rooted in ethnicity (Wan & Casey, 2014, p. 108). In a small or medium sized city, newly arrived immigrants and recently resettled refugees may live in the same apartment complex and, although they come from vastly different parts of the world, they discover that they share many common needs and challenges as minorities in the dominant American culture of their new city. This commonality may represent the genesis of a new "urban tribe."

As New York City missionaries, we refer to one of our ministry's demographics as "native Bronx." These ministry clusters include Italian, Puerto Rican, Dominican, Irish, East European, or any variety of cultural backgrounds. They are often the second or third generation of immigrants living between the worlds of either current or fading ethnic enclaves and the wider urban culture beyond those enclaves, but we have also experienced these multiethnic clusters as a mix of highly assimilated first generation immigrants combined with second generation individuals and connecting as a single ethnically diverse network or community. They are not simply fully assimilated immigrants. On the contrary, these multiethnic clusters are often distinct subcultures within the fabric of the city. While creating a new multiethnic subculture, they often maintain ties to their culture of origin (or parent's ethnic culture) as well. These multiethnic clusters maintain relational links to specific cultural networks, neighborhoods, or family groups. Some will only exist in the new subculture, but many will live between both worlds. They represent bridges between difficult cultural spheres spending the majority of their time in their multiethnic urban subculture but retain ties and interact sporadically with a homogenous ethnic community as well. Maintaining these multiple identities is part of their everyday life.

Many individuals simultaneously operate in two or three of these cultural spheres described above. They have flexible cultural identities that allow them to move between cultural communities. Members of a "new urban tribe" may also function, to varying degrees, within an enclave or network as well as cultivating a sense of belonging in a multiethnic community. These are bridge people that have relationships and personal histories in an ethnic enclave, have stayed connected with their larger ethnic network in a city through family connections, and have partially assimilated by joining a new multiethnic subculture. Such individuals have acquired the ability, usually through raw life experiences, to move fluidly between cultural worlds within a city. For the cross-cultural evangelist, it is important to recognize that building trust with one individual may actually connect them to multiple cultural spheres in the city, and perhaps even globally to their countries of origin. These individuals also possess the innate ability to move between cultural spheres—an essential quality for the next generation of Christian leaders serving a global society.

An example from our work might serve to illustrate the complexity and fluidity of the urban tribe. First, we might consider one of the initial church groups that I (Seth) worked with in the Bronx. In our work, we seek what we call "people of peace"—that is, people who seem receptive to our evangelistic message—encouraging them to gather their households to study Scripture together. In this instance, the person of peace was a second-generation Italian and former Catholic turned New Age advisor. The "household" he gathered included a Gnostic Jewish acquaintance with his Puerto Rican slam-poet friend; an Italian co-worker who attended Tai-Chi lessons with him; this coworker's first-generation Turkish neighbor (a practicing Buddhist); the same coworker's girlfriend who was a first generation Eritrean and was a part of a "goddess" religious movement; and a Montenegrin ex-Muslim he knew from his gym. These individuals all knew one another and considered each other to be their primary community, despite the fact that they each have larger family networks in the immediate area whose cultural worlds they navigate with equal mastery to their constructed tribal hybrid.

These three patterns obviously hold great potential for overlap and interconnection. They represent different ways that diaspora communities might be structured around an ethnic identity, a geographic zone with clear cultural boundaries, and/or a common affinity, but it is important to recognize that they point to diverse possibilities in terms of ministry plans as well. If our desire is to impact the nations in our cities, it is important to recognize that we are not advocating a one-size-fits-all approach. Rather we hope to offer a process of thinking about the multiple responses to the varied realities reflected in the networks and neighborhoods in our cities. We also have no intention for any of these ideas to represent prescriptive recipes for ministry success. Rather, we hope to aid the creative process by offering frameworks and options for thinking strategically about Kingdom impact in our cities.

Local Churches and Ministry Approaches

As Christian ministries begin to consider how they might reach out to an international community within their city, it is important to highlight that there are multiple options. In doing so, we are emphasizing that the different cultural realities in a given location will have an influence on our ministry choices. In most cases in large cities, each of the cultural profiles explained previously will be present. This means that many churches, church planters, or outreach organizations have the option of focusing on a narrow niche and limiting themselves to one or perhaps only a few profiles, while other churches will want to push the span of their ministry reach to the greatest cultural distance possible. Again, we want to emphasize that there is a need both for deep specialization and for long-reaching, broad vision. The internal ministry context will matter as well. Smaller churches may seek to do one or two things well while larger churches may have the capacity and the resources to sustain multiple concurrent ministry platforms. Likewise, a cluster of smaller churches may partner together in order to resource a larger initiative among one or more cultural groups in their city.

When you are discerning the ministry approach that will make the most impact in your city, two key considerations are: (a) the cultural context of the particular community or communities that you are encountering, and (b) accessing the resources and potentials within your church or team. Are you interacting with a tightly connected ethnic network that stretches across the city, a distinct geographic zone or ethnic neighborhood within your city, new subcultures of highly assimilated first generation immigrants and/or second generation immigrants, or some combination of two or more of these community profiles? In addition, what are the particular human resources and capacities of your church or organization? Simply put, what do you have to work with? You may have a big vision, but you have to start with what you have.

Invitations and Hospitality

The most obvious plan for most churches is to invite their new international neighbors to worship with their church. That is in fact a much-needed practice for many churches. First, many immigrants are already Christians or, though not yet committed to Christian faith, were educated in church-based schools or other Christian community service programs in their countries of origin. Often, these churches have been shaped, intentionally or unintentionally, by Western influences, so these individuals feel quite at home in the typical church in the United States. In addition, some non-Christian immigrants are eager to assimilate to the dominant culture, and are pleased to receive an invitation to visit or join an American institution even if it involves exploring a new religion. Quite a few new international neighbors are happy to attend an American church and learn new ideas in this type of setting. Christians transferring from overseas churches, non-Christians who have had pleasant experiences in Western-style churches before coming to the United States, and non-Christians who are especially eager to assimilate with the dominant Western culture, as well as any number of cultural anomalies, are all potential visitors to North American churches in their city. Finding a hospitable Christian community will be a reason for celebration for these individuals and families.

One of the most profound ministries that a church may offer is the service of hospitality. Many immigrants arrive in U.S. cities only to confront numerous challenges and an uphill battle to establish themselves and their families in their new environment. They may experience culture shock, an anti-immigrant bias, or even racism upon arriving in their new city. Finding a welcoming community instead of rejection expresses a love and compassion which embodies the heart of the Gospel, echoing Jesus's teaching: "I was a stranger, and you invited me in" (Mt. 25:35). Whatever an immigrant's motivation for connecting with a Christian church, an accepted invitation to church opens a window of opportunity to express the love of Christ.

Multi-Congregational Churches

The multi-congregational approach is similar to a single congregation inviting their international neighbors to their church; however, there is an intentional effort to structure organizational and congregational life to account for multiple subcultures or linguistic groupings. These churches invite new immigrants to an established religious space, but the multi-congregational approach allows the church's ministry to be offered in diverse languages and styles of worship under the umbrella of a shared ministry in the same facility.

There are generally three approaches to multi-congregational churches. First, in the "rented space" model, the relationship between the congregations is limited to a business arrangement in which a culturally different church rents the facilities for their own worship services. A second multi-congregational scenario is when a church welcomes a culturally different congregation to share their space, with the caveat that the welcoming church remains in authority. The hosting church publically celebrates the use of their facility by the culturally different congregation, but the guest congregation remains a borrower in the relationship. Finally, in a more integrative approach the culturally different congregations see themselves as one church. They share responsibility for the church and its resources as a shared ministry, and they share authority as a leadership team working together while caring for different language or cultural congregations within the church (Ortiz, 1996, pp. 66–78).

It is fairly commonplace to share physical space with another congregation meeting in a different language in the same facility. One of the weaknesses of this approach emerges when the congregation that owns the building treats the guest congregation as second-class members rather than ministry partners working to reach different cultural and lingual demographics. There are countless scenarios in which the basis for the relationship is rooted in one church approaching another with the hopes of renting their facility, and the openness to renting unused space to a culturally different congregation ultimately should be applauded. However, if the leaders of both congregations take a more integrated approach, working together as co-leaders or partners, they often are able to minister more effectively to the second-generation within their shared community.

I (Jared) first encountered this approach when serving with a multiethnic ministry in Houston several years ago. We had two congregations, one worshipping in English and the other in Spanish, cooperating closely as a single leadership team. The English-speaking and Spanish-speaking leaders functioned as one leadership, and elders for the church as a whole were drawn from both congregations. As a result, the second-generation children were able to integrate into a common youth ministry, typically in English. Since then, I have seen this multi-congregational approach provide an effective platform for retaining and/or reaching the second generation immigrant children in their church in various ministry settings in New York City. In a fully integrated multi-congregational church, leaders work together on a united front with each focusing their primary efforts within their cultural group.

The multi-congregational approach may be helpful for established congregations to consider, especially if they own a large facility space that is under-utilized. This style of ministry will not reach every immigrant community, but it may be effective at making an impact among immigrant households that are already comfortable with American styles of church but still desire to function within their own primary culture or first language. This approach works best when there is shared leadership and mutual collaboration between the different linguistic communities. However, a congregation may extend a warm welcome to a culturally different congregation borrowing or leasing space. This will often be the initial approach for churches just beginning to explore these options while both working in the same area of the city. Churches may initially decide to share space and then move through a process of greater integration. As different cultural communities begin to explore working together, most diaspora congregations will include English speakers, although it would be wise for at least one American leader in the church to begin learning the language of the ethnic congregation as well. This strengthens the bridges between congregations within the church and demonstrates respect and admiration for our international brothers and sisters.

Planting Churches

In our experience in large cities, a dynamic large church with abundant ministry programs commonly sits near a large ethnic enclave with few if any from that diaspora community attending the church. Despite the geographic proximity, the cultural distance is huge. Simply being physically close does not mean that our diaspora neighbors necessarily will be attracted to our church's activities. In order to reach the majority of immigrant households in our cities, there is quite often a need for contextualized church planting among specific cultural networks and neighborhood enclaves as well as in multiethnic communities that remain distant, culturally or theologically, from any sort of Christian community. We highly recommend considering alternative strategies for church planting when initiating cross-cultural ministry to find those that are most congruent to the specific culture(s) in your situation.

Many churches will feel under-resourced if their vision is to plant a new church cross-culturally. The real issue, however, may be that the church itself has a limited view of the variety of strategic possibilities for starting churches. The quintessential American approach of launching an inaugural service after an aggressive advertising campaign may even backfire if the ministry is seeking to evangelize an unreached or resistant ethnic group. It may signal that the community is a target and prompt their religious leaders to begin warning their adherents about the impending church planting effort. In contrast, starting small churches in homes and places of business allows church planting to begin with low financial requirements and, if necessary, a low public profile. Planting small churches also allows Christian workers to begin their outreach efforts at a foundational level without imposing further cultural adjustments to the already-disoriented lives of immigrants.

By beginning with a small group and building trust, the Christian worker assists the new believers in establishing best practices for worship, evangelism, or leadership development within their own cultural realities. Small, contextualized church planting offers increased opportunity for evangelism and additional church planting to expand through the effort of emerging leaders from within the diaspora community, as they are empowered to make many of the decisions concerning contextualization themselves. While we advocate a ministry strategy directed towards multiplying many smaller communities, house churches may either continue to multiply, or they may decide to combine into larger churches. Regardless of the strategic outcome, this allows for the time and intentionality needed to develop communities of faith from the ground up in partnership with diaspora leaders within the community. This approach to church planting requires a more modest beginning with a slower ramp-up; however, by refraining from rushing diaspora believers into standard American practices, it provides time to work in partnership with our diaspora neighbors to discover which practices will lead to a deep Gospel impact among the unreached in the community.

Church planting, as compared to assimilating immigrants into existing congregations, allows for the greatest degree of contextualization. Ethnic others do not have to enter an essentially American space that is foreign to them in order to hear the proclamation of the Gospel. New believers may develop as disciples of Christ while feeling culturally at home. Evangelism approaches, expressions of worship, teaching styles, symbolism, leadership, and similar elements of Christian practices are all tailored to the preferences of the particular ethnic and linguistic community. In many cases such contextualization will be essential for the greatest Gospel impact. Cross-culturally planting new churches in ethnic neighborhoods or networks creates the space for deeply contextualizing Christian practices among a particular cultural group and to address the myths and behaviors of the immediate culture.

Cultural Satellites

Alternative outreach platforms provide a fourth option for Christian leaders considering how they might reach out cross-culturally in their city. In recent years, it has become popular for growing churches to establish satellite congregations. Usually these additional campuses are similar, if not identical, to the cultural makeup of the mother congregation and they stream video versions of the preaching for their satellite congregations to hear the same message as their congregational headquarters. We are not advocating this pattern of satellites for cross-cultural outreach; however, a similar approach may provide an avenue for mobilizing growing churches for cross-cultural ministry in their city. A culturally distinct satellite approach may provide an alternative platform for cross-cultural outreach. This approach may represent a compromise or hybrid on the continuum between church planting and multi-congregational churches.

This approach would allow a church the opportunity to initiate a cross-cultural outreach to first generation immigrants without forcing them into a culturally foreign space. Rather than a video stream to a culturally identical satellite, the church leadership sponsors an off-campus outreach ministry that reflects the culture of the immigrant community. A church may design a café intended to connect with Muslims who would be unlikely to visit their church space. They may launch a Spanish-language assembly off-site from their campus in the heart of the Latino community and allow it to develop worship and preaching styles that are congruent to the cultural flavors of the community. The church may sponsor a friendship center: a space designed to welcome the city's newest immigrants, teach ESL, offer legal services, and provide refugees with some basic necessities. There are a variety of options for developing this sort of platform. By establishing an off-campus satellite, the sponsoring church may continue to invest directly in the community and mobilize their church for cross-cultural outreach while allowing the satellite ministry to flourish with cultural autonomy within their diaspora context.

In addition, small cells meeting in homes, not unlike house churches, could be planted but maintain connections under the umbrella of the leadership of the sponsoring congregation. This approach would be different from a typical cell church model in that the individual groups would have more independence than traditional small groups. They would function more like house churches but maintain ties to the central leadership of the sponsoring church. The leaders of a satellite or home fellowship may participate in the leadership structure of the larger church but continue leading a community of faith in a context that is culturally, geographically, and linguistically distinct. There are a variety of possibilities for establishing cultural satellites that may provide a pathway for churches to reach out to culturally different communities beyond their immediate physical space.

These ministries would be considered satellites because they are off-site from the main campus but are still sponsored by the church leadership. However, they do not participate in video streaming or similar connections that would be culturally foreign to their faith formation in the diaspora context. One of the weaknesses of this approach, however, might be the tendency for the central leadership to become paternalistic about a ministry that is culturally different but ultimately still under their authority. The danger of colonialism has a way of creeping into even the local "mission field." Another danger is the tendency to see this ministry as nothing more than a line on a budget whose disappearance would likely have little effect on the main campus. Cross-cultural ministry can certainly present a conundrum for the theological priorities of ministry leaders.

On the other hand, if a church sponsors a cultural satellite conscientiously, a healthy partnership may emerge. The congregation may function similarly to an integrated multi-congregational church, utilizing a decentralized organizational model with an incarnational presence within the local diaspora community. Also, one of the strengths of this approach would be that churches still exploring long term plans for church planting ministry may launch a cultural satellite as an interim strategy. Often the urgency for evangelism and church planting efforts in ethnic communities outpaces the readiness of a church's leadership to dive into cross-cultural ministry. Sometimes new waves of immigrants or large numbers of refugees arrive in a city with little time for local churches to prepare a "game plan." Sometimes an interim strategy is needed as way to respond to the urgency of new ministry opportunities.

For this reason, a cultural satellite may be advantageous, given the way it allows a sponsoring church to take time to develop self-sustaining leadership practices before releasing the satellite as a new church plant. It may act as a feeder for the larger church, as some immigrants who initially were reluctant to join an American church develop a desire to do so as they assimilate to the dominant culture and want their children to grow up in it. The cultural satellite provides a natural bridge for this transition into the larger faith community. In other cases, of course, a cultural satellite may continue as an arm of the sponsoring church's ministry indefinitely, much like a multi-congregational model.

Practice

As you discern your ministry approach, we recommend that you ask the following questions. While they need not be mutually exclusive, it is important to prioritize to ensure that you and your team move forward with a clear and cogent strategy. In this exercise, reflect on the following questions in regards to how important each will be in regards to forming your ministry approach.

1. What is the most incarnational approach for reaching our neighbor?
2. What successful ministries are already being done among our neighbors, and could we partner with them?
3. What are acceptable outcomes given the resources we intend to expend?
4. To what extent will the church membership be active in this ministry?
5. What structures would we have to create or adapt to integrate another culture successfully into our existing ministries?
6. If this ministry is being primarily led or conducted by lay members of your church, what structures of training, accountability, and pastoral care must we create or adapt to support this work?

Chapter 5

Preserving Identity in a Global World

A common assumption is that recent immigrants are likely to respond well to the message of the Gospel. We might contend that "people tend to be more receptive to the Gospel when they are in times of stress and transition, both situations very common among migrants" (Payne, 2012, p. 131). This is true in a number of circumstances. Many of our diaspora neighbors, while living in transition between cultures, are more open to discussing new ideas, including the Gospel of Christ. We want to celebrate this opportunity within close reach to Christ's body in North American cities.

At the same time, we have also encountered a number of migrants from various parts of the world who cling dogmatically to their traditional beliefs, customs, and cultural narratives. When I (Seth) was doing my initial ethnographic work in the Bengali community in the Bronx, I remember asking a friend about the normative dress for men. I had noticed that many Bengali men who were middle aged and older wore similar hats and dyed their beards an orange hue. When I asked my friend Hasan the reason for doing this he replied, "It is because of the prophet." I asked him whether the prophet Mohammad had done these same things. Hasan did not know. I asked him whether the prophet had commanded others to do these things. He did not know. "What does it mean, then," I asked him, "to do these things 'because of the prophet?'" He replied firmly, "We do them because of the prophet." As in every culture, the reasons and meaning of certain behaviors is forgotten over time. This should not, suggest, however that the behaviors themselves lose value. For some international migrants, their religious identity—if tied to their cultural heritage—can become more meaningful to them as they move into a diaspora community far from their homeland (Warner & Wittner, 1998, p. 3).

By this conservationist mentality, some immigrants seek to preserve identity in the midst of enormous change and find stability in a cultural-religious home. A trait of urban environments often overlooked by church planting strategists is that multiple contradictory processes often occur simultaneously. Within a diaspora population, some pockets may be extremely open to new ideas—including giving a fair hearing to the good news of God's Kingdom—while other pockets in the same community aggressively defend their cultural and religious heritage. This also explains why some diaspora neighbors will be eager to visit an American church, while reaching out to others may require a highly contextualized approach. In order to navigate these contrasting responses to migration and cultural diversity, Christian leaders will need to listen diligently and practice pastoral sensitivity as essential disciplines for our evangelistic efforts.

For these reasons, it will be helpful for us look into some of the psychology behind transition and mental stress. Cognitive dissonance theory teaches that when a person's experience brings two incompatible beliefs or identities into conflict, the person will seek resolution to this psychological tension (Festinger, Riecken, & Schachter, 2009). This resolution generally happens in one of three ways: First, a person may change or abandon one of the beliefs; second, they may develop or add new beliefs which help to support what is already believed; or, third, they may decrease the perceived importance of the belief in question. After expending mental and emotional energy to affect the value of a belief, a person may experience "effort justification," a phenomenon in which this result—be it the retention or changing of this belief—is perceived as being of greater value than the previous state, thereby reducing cognitive dissonance (Maich, 2014, p. 1). It is helpful for us to realize the inherent stress that takes place both during the conversion process as well as the journey of international migration.

It is also important to note that cognitive dissonance, while stressful, is often an unconscious experience. An internal stress may be present in our friend, but they may not understand the root causes of their sense of dissonance or be unable to articulate them. Alternatively, we may be inaccurately attributing signs in our neighbor of fatigue or stress to cognitive dissonance when in reality they are struggling through some other factors that are creating emotional pain. For these reasons, we must be sensitive to not draw attention to cognitive dissonance when we see (or suspect that we see) it happening in the lives of those around us. Our evangelism may benefit from being aware the emotional processes which emerge from cognitive dissonance, but when encountering it in our friends, quiet pastoral concern and a listening ear are most likely the best responses.

When considering cognitive dissonance among international diaspora, we might take my (Seth's) friend Ali as an example. For some time Ali attended a house-church and was engaged in one of our evangelistic Bible studies. Despite his regular attendance, Ali never missed an opportunity to share his opinion that all religious beliefs were a waste of time and that religious people were intellectually inferior. When I (Seth) began to discuss his back-story with him, I learned that Ali was born into a large Bosnian Muslim family. As a teenager, he had begun to question his faith and this had caused a rift in his relationship with his family. He was ridiculed and isolated, although eventually a shaky relationship with his family.was restored. Because of his experience of cognitive dissonance with leaving Islam, Ali, by his own admission, does not believe it is rational to pursue learning or understanding alternative religions. Because he suffered for leaving his faith behind, he does not believe it would be valuable to now invest effort into pursuing another faith.

Applying cognitive dissonance theory to Ali's story, we might say that this is a manifestation of effort justification. When Ali comes to our church and reads and discusses Scripture with us his decision to leave Islam is brought back into dissonance: If he is considering religion again, does that make his painful decision in the past less meaningful or even risk rendering it meaningless? Cognitive dissonance theory would tell us that his desire to justify to himself and others his decision to reject religion is a manifestation of Ali's cognitive dissonance. When we are helping people understand the Gospel of Christ, dissonance may be common, and pastoral sensitivity is often required as individuals walk through the process of wrestling with the teachings of the Bible. If we are honest about our own experiences, turning one's allegiance to Christ is often a *process* rather than *an event* of conversion. We should expect dissonance to be a common experience during this process and care for our friends accordingly.

Mosaic

On the other side of the spectrum we might apply cognitive dissonance theory to help understand my friend Tash. Although he came to the US from Bangladesh early in his life, Tash's life experiences correspond closely to that of second generation immigrants: He came up through American schools, has always spoken English, and has been able to form relationships easily in the wider culture outside of the Bengali community. Earlier this year, however, Tash moved from his affluent neighborhood in Manhattan into a mostly Bengali community in the Bronx. He does not want his wife and children to have to live outside of Bengali culture any more than is necessary, and he wants to limit the influence of American morals on his family.

Cognitive dissonance theory would explain Tash's actions as follows: Given the degree of assimilation which he has already undergone, those elements of his native culture which he has preserved are precious to him and thus, because of effort justification, are all the more valued. This being the case, he protects the remaining facets of his cultural identity—particularly as expressed through his religious observance—and seeks to avoid any further experiences of dissonance. It may be helpful to know that, despite his being second generation in the immigration cycle, Tash is one of the most faithful practitioners of Islam we know among Bengalis in the Bronx. Religion has become a way to hold onto his cultural identity.

For almost every individual in the diaspora, cognitive dissonance is just another part of the immigration process. The first in the family to immigrate moves into an apartment—often with several other first generation immigrants from their home country— while saving enough money to bring their immediate families to the United

States and then their parents and extended family. After immigration, each of these individuals has a different experience of assimilation and continues on that trajectory through the course of their life in this new home.

Often, "the timeframe for assimilation extends across generations" (Scott, Agnew, Soja, & Storper, 2001, p. 312). This means that immigration brings about the intersection of many myths and experiences central to both a person's home culture and the new culture and that, after undergoing the normative immigrant experience of dissonance, an individual might create any number of hybrid narratives which we would not expect to see in either their culture of origin or the dominant host culture. As new cultural attributes are gained, other cultural traits are lost and a degree of cultural mixing occurs, a process of "cultural building" often takes place among diaspora communities (Rynkiewich, 2012, p. 210). This third culture phenomenon makes it even more essential that we deeply examine both our own culture and that of our friends in the diaspora in order to contextualize the Gospel adequately. Speaking to our international neighbors, we cannot assume that they embody a worldview that represents a completely American perspective. Neither should we expect that they have maintained the worldviews of their homeland in totality. Often they are living between cultural worlds. While some individuals or families are a greater reflection of their culture of origin, others have moved closer to the new host culture. Still others may represent a significant merger of cultural worlds.

Practice One

Case Study

In Bangladesh, many important decisions are made by respected older men who, after entering semi-retirement, have lots of time to study the holy texts and consult with one another regarding community affairs. However, after moving to the U.S., these devout elders have found that the positions of authority they possessed back home have been filled by local Bengali business owners who employ the majority of the diaspora community. These younger businessmen are generally far less devout than their elders, but their social utility for economic advancement is considered more primary in the immigrant community. Perhaps out of resentment, the elders hold up their religiosity like an accusation against the increasingly nominal community. When asked about the issue, the commercial leaders of the community accuse the elders of having "nothing to do but go to *Masjid* and discuss the prophet while they grow out their beards." This is not meant as a compliment in their new home.

Using your understanding of cognitive dissonance discussed in this chapter, identify the pertinent issues on both sides of this dispute and the different ways that you might present the Gospel to each party. Discuss how you might utilize the tension between the Pharisees and "sinners" of the Jewish diaspora in the Gospels as a parallel to help share the story of Jesus within this diaspora neighbor's community:

Notes:

Practice Two

Case Study

You are invited to celebrate Durga puja, a Hindu holiday and
the biggest celebration connected to the Hindu god Durga, with your
friend Tanei. You have shared your Christian faith with Tanei many
times and have established an ongoing friendship. Through your
conversations and time with his family, you are continually learning
about potential bridges and apparent barriers for communicating the
Gospel with your Hindu friend. As you believe that this is a good
opportunity to learn about your Hindu friend's culture and its religious
influences and since you do not believe that there will be any pressure
for you to actually worship idols in any way by just attending the
festival, you agree to go. Over the course of the night you try to engage
Tanei with your questions about the meaning of various elements of
the celebration, particularly about the relationship between Durga and
the other Hindu gods. You know that Tanei and his family are
primarily Krishna devotees, so you ask about Krishna's status in
relation to Durga. "We call him, *Lord* Krishna," Tanei corrects you,
sternly. You have discussed Hindu beliefs in Krishna many times in the
past, and he has never at any time before insisted on this formal title in
previous religious conversations between the two of you. It is rare that
you see him this severe and it is obvious that he wants you to use the
same formal title, "Lord Krishna."

1. What questions do you need to ask in order to move forward in
   your conversation?

2. Knowing that you have had previous discussions about Krishna with Tanei without needing to include a title, use your knowledge from the previous chapters to explain why you think attending Durga puja has changed Tanei's intensity regarding religious reverence.

3. How can you use this as an opportunity to learn more about myths concerning "Lordship" in Hindu culture and how might you turn this interaction around to make a statement about Christ as Lord without offending your host and permanently damaging your friendship?

Notes:

Chapter 6

Levels of Observation

Levels of Observation for the Cultural Hosts

After understanding the role of myth and narrative in cultural identity and integrating that knowledge into the complex framework of assimilation, let us further explain the picture by acknowledging the larger network of observation that takes place in ministering cross-culturally. In any evangelistic work, but especially when we are working with communal cultures, we must keep in mind that nothing we say or do is received or reviewed by only the intended audience. Even in the most private of circumstances, our comments, stories, and actions may be shared by our international friends with their families once we are no longer present. Far more commonly, we will be sharing the Gospel with a particular individual while several others listen in. We must account for this ripple effect in our contextualization, using these concentric circles of observation wisely for the spread of the Gospel.

Take for example one of our missionary's experiences of teaching English in the home of a Bengali woman in the Bronx. Hardly a week goes by that her host, Kala, does not invite another friend or two over for their language practice. Often if there is no other guest invited, Kala will Skype her husband who lives back in Bangladesh while the missionary is in her home. This has often led to opportunities to communicate the Gospel through technology with her family in Bangladesh. While Kala is Hindu, since she lives in a Muslim-majority neighborhood, frequently the friends who attend are Muslims. Any statement of faith is then open to being processed through multiple spheres of observation: it cuts across levels of intimacy as strangers hear the message across gender and across multiple religious identities. Not only that, it is being heard and interpreted both in a living room in New York City and in front of a computer screen in South Asia. Is there a way to make a statement of faith that can address all of these issues of contextualization? What are the problems involved?

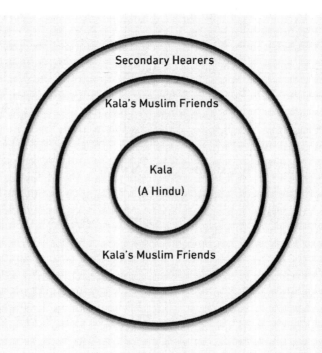

Gate-keepers and Cultural informants

Another factor to consider in roles of observation are relationships that help you learn about and navigate your diaspora neighbors' culture but who may or may not themselves be receptive to the Gospel. In our work we generally identify two such categories of relationship referred to by function: gatekeeper and cultural informant. Gatekeepers are individuals who control access to a wider network of relationships. They could be key business owners within a diaspora community, the Latina matriarch of a large family, an apartment building superintendent or the bartender at the local pub— basically whoever can open doors of relationship and credibility within the community is a gatekeeper.

Gatekeepers have the ability to open networks of relationships without necessarily being spiritually receptive themselves. The important aspect of gatekeeper relationships is that they are open to you as the messenger. Although they may or may not be spiritually open to your message, it is important that gatekeepers understand your identity as a follower of Jesus as they open the door for additional relationships through their influence in the community. It is better to be open about our relationship to Christ in a culturally sensitive way early in the friendship rather than risk creating a "bait and switch" situation that could backfire later. Our friend is allowing us to use his or her influence and connections to gain access to their network of relationships. We do not want to abuse their trust by misrepresenting ourselves or our intentions. Being honest with a gatekeeper who is open to us as the messenger may result in even greater access as trust grows and the relationship develops.

Mosaic

A good example of a gatekeeper in our work would be my (Seth's) friend Gary. Gary is one of the most successful business owners in my neighborhood, having run a successful and honest auto shop for almost 30 years in the same location. Everyone in the area knows this shop and trusts the employees because of Gary's reputation for doing quality work at a fair price. While Gary has never shown any interest in the stories I share about Jesus, it is a rare month when he does not invite me out with a group of his friends, praising me as "a Christian like you've never met before." He tells them, "This guy will make you think differently about religion." In this way, despite his own lack of spiritual interest, Gary has facilitated my connection with dozens of people who were interested in what we had to share, all the more so because of Gary's endorsement of me as a trustworthy person.

Cultural informants may or may not be the same individual as a gatekeeper. These individuals play a key role in helping us understand the culture we are attempting to serve. As the name suggests, they provide answers for our many questions about the culture, but also forgiveness for the inevitable faux pas which are the norm for any new cross-cultural minister. Cross-cultural evangelists must never be so paralyzed by fear of doing or saying the wrong thing that we fail to try; however, it is equally important that we find cultural informants to debrief our missteps in a new culture. Unlike gatekeepers, who may be few and far between, it is likely that we will find as many cultural informants as there are sub-cultures in the community.

It is wise to bring up information gleaned from one cultural informant in conversation with another in order to confirm this information. In a diaspora community in the city, residents may have originated from different regions with different cultural assumptions even when migrating from the same country of origin to the same neighborhood. In addition, the immigrant community as a whole is on a continuum of assimilation (Looney, 2015, pp. 187–192). Some are more socialized to the dominant American culture while others are holding steadfastly to the cultural norms of the homeland. Getting a "second opinion" from another informant will help us verify what we have learned and provide a more nuanced understanding of the relationship between various elements of an ethnic community.

Some of the best cultural informants are individuals who are marginal to their own cultural centers. While it is easy to lack perspective or not consider critically much of what is "normal" to one's own way of life, those who have been excluded or marginalized often do not take as much for granted about their community as others do. Thus, they may be able to explain many things in terms more helpful than "that is just the way things are done." It is also important to note that while a relationship with a gate-keeper is likely to raise one's status in the eyes of the community, one's status may be lowered for publically engaging a cultural informant in friendship, depending on the reasons for their marginalization. Whether this makes the relationship a threat to one's ministry or an opportunity to witness to the Gospel is, of course, left to the discretion of the minister and highlights the need for discernment on a case-by-case basis.

Practice One

Case Study

You have an evangelistic Bible study with two men: one is half Italian and half Puerto Rican and left the Catholic church at age twelve, the other is Turkish and grew up in a completely secular home but became a practitioner of Zen Buddhism in his twenties. Both are highly relativistic in their worldview and prone to distrust anyone who speaks about their beliefs as if they follow the only true religion. You have had success presenting the Gospel to them as a way of life that Jesus challenges people to put into practice (particularly as we see in the Sermon on the Mount). You have encouraged them to judge from experience whether or not it is the most fulfilling way to live, hoping that as they continue to follow the practices of the life of a disciple, the Holy Spirit and the challenge of Scripture will begin to reshape broken elements of their worldview. Contextually this approach, as a beginning point, seems to suit their myths about truth as a pragmatic rather than an objective value.

Recently, they have developed a love for Bengali food. A Bengali restaurant where you are reasonably well known is near the house of your Turkish friend. They have moved the location of your Bible study to this restaurant for the foreseeable future. Evening is the busiest time in the Bengali community as many of the men, drink tea and debate various matters of importance for several hours after work. Sharing the Gospel with a small group made up of a Zen Buddhist and a nominal Catholic would likely require a different approach than speaking with a group of South Asian Muslims. However, the tables are at close quarters so everything you discuss with your friends is likely to be overheard. Using your knowledge from the previous chapters, identify the issues of contextualization and levels of observation involved and how you would handle the situation.

Notes:

Practice Two

Case Study

A relative of your Hindu friend has passed away and you are invited to the funeral. The ceremony takes place over several nights in various locations, all of them in the Indian neighborhood where you live. For the first two nights of the funeral you are allowed to sit in as a casual observer but are not expected to do more than eat with the family and quietly watch the prayers and ritual. On the last night you accept the final invitation to the funeral activities and find yourself attending the final ceremony, which includes meat offered to the Hindu idol and a man circling the room and marking the forehead of every person with a painted dot. You had noticed earlier in the night that none of your Muslim friends attended this meeting, although a few had come to pay their respects on the previous nights. You also will have to walk home when the funeral is over, potentially passing Muslim friends as well as your Central American neighbors with whom you have been openly sharing the Gospel. At this point in the evening, it is still early enough to depart without causing offense to your hosts. As you consider this dilemma, how do you decide whether or not to stay for the remainder of the evening? What are the risks involved with the decision to stay or to leave? Compare the different nights in regards to the levels of observation involved.

Notes:

Looney & Bouchelle

Chapter 7

Contextualization vs. Syncretism

Contextualization is not a choice. When each of us first heard the Gospel, it was presented to us in the context of our own culture, and most of us continued to live out its application in culturally familiar settings. The Gospel presents itself to us through Scripture as a message contextualized to the first hearers, and we came to understand it as it was re-contextualized in our culture. If this were not the case, we would be unable to expand our understanding of discipleship and God's Kingdom to include contemporary changes in our world: our ability to apply the Gospel to family when American families are no longer multi-generational within the same household as they were in the first century; our ability to explain the atonement in a culture which does not practice animal sacrifice; our understanding of the role of Christians within a democracy; or our discernment of the ways in which Christians should engage Muslims or Mormons as they make competing claims about the identity of Jesus—all of these are issues of contextualization we have had to work through as contemporary American Christians.

Contextualization does not mean a change of the Gospel, but it affects how the Gospel engages people within their respective cultures. It represents an expanded application and interpretation of the principles of the Gospel to engage a changing culture. The Gospel was

135

first proclaimed within the context of the first century Mediterranean world. When we apply these truths to the radically different cultural settings in which we live today, we are contextualizing the message into our own cultural setting, whether or not we recognize that we are doing so. Not to engage actively in contextualization on matters such as these is not to allow for the expansion of the Gospel to meet issues that exist in modern culture but not in the culture of the writers of Scripture. If we cannot adapt the presentation of the Gospel to every culture, we separate it from the character of God, whose essential nature is incarnational.

When we refuse to allow the Gospel to contextualize to the culture we are sharing with, we choose to leave it in the state in which it was initially contextualized to us within our own culture. The Gospel always functions within culture. We received the Gospel within our culture and our own language. It was communicated in a way that made sense to us, but in that form it may or may not make sense to someone of another culture. At its heart, this denial of context does not represent a preservation of the Gospel, but a refusal to allow the message of God's Kingdom to incarnate itself into cultures other than our own.

Historically, Christians from Western cultures have overlooked the need for contextualized communication of the Gospel. Refusing to see beyond our own cultural boundaries, the Christian church expanded with language and structures formed through exclusively Western experiences. Lack of effort in contextualization led to two consequences. First, people of other nations tended to view Christianity as a foreign intrusion, rather than a faith relevant to their own culture. Secondly, non-Christian beliefs and practices continued to exist below the surface of "accepted" Western Christianity. Because they were not openly engaged by the Gospel, these elements of their indigenous faith systems simply went "underground" (Hiebert, 1987, p. 106). As our cities increasingly represent a global social context, we have much to learn from such historical missteps.

The question is not "Should we contextualize?" but "How do we contextualize faithfully?" Intentionally or unintentionally, we *will* communicate the Gospel through some kind of cultural filter. Good contextualization occurs when we manage to separate the message of the Gospel from our own culture without supplanting the values of the Kingdom for those of the receiving culture. This requires that we allow the Gospel to confront opposing values in the receiving culture but that we also allow values compatible with the Gospel to remain. As cross-cultural leaders, we have the opportunity to incorporate the missionary practice of "critical contextualization" into our ministry strategy.

While exact application may vary by circumstance, Paul Hiebert explains the basic approach of critical contextualization as a four-stage process. First, we seek to understand the culture. During this part of the process, we withhold judgment while we seek to learn all we can about the existing religious beliefs and customs of a people. Second, the cross-cultural missionary assists the community of believers to study the Scriptures regarding questions arising from their own context. Thirdly, the community itself critically evaluates pre-existing practices or customs in light of their growing understanding of biblical teachings. Finally, the community can adapt old practices or form new practices and rituals that suit their own cultural context (Hiebert, 1987, pp. 109–110). The diversity we encounter in multicultural cities and in diaspora networks necessitates that cross-cultural evangelists work with sensitivity and nuance. However, Hiebert's template of critical contextualization provides us with a general framework of principles for thinking about ministry outside of our own cultural world.

As evangelists, we are seeking to help people grow to be more like Christ, not more like ourselves. This requires two disciplined practices:

1. We must allow the Gospel to speak to things that it does not necessarily speak to in our own cultural context.
2. We must allow the Gospel to speak only to what it does and not to what we *wish* it might due to our own cultural assumptions.

We cannot force the Gospel to say what it does not, nor should we fail to let it address what it wishes to across the diverse spectrum of culture. So, for example, with many of my (Seth) Bengali friends, the Gospel must address the role of idol worship and caste, neither of which exist explicitly in my own culture. Failure to let the Gospel address these practices, either out of fear that it will be rejected or ignorance caused by my own cultural blindness, is a failure to fully embody the message of Jesus Christ. But in relation to the institution of arranged marriages in Bengali culture, the Gospel is not undermined by this cultural practice and my own cultural assumptions about how couples pursue marriage are not explicitly addressed in the Gospel. It would therefore be wrong for me to present those cultural beliefs as a facet of the good news of Jesus.

Failure to contextualize the Gospel appropriately is called syncretism. Syncretism occurs when we bend the Gospel to accommodate beliefs or practices that it otherwise might have opposed or when we force the Gospel to speak to what is outside of its mission. In syncretism, core Christian beliefs or practices are blended with non-

Christian beliefs or practices so that the heart of the Gospel is lost. Good contextualization is opposed to syncretism. To avoid syncretism is to not only recognize the pitfalls that might be present in our diaspora neighbors' culture, but also in our own.

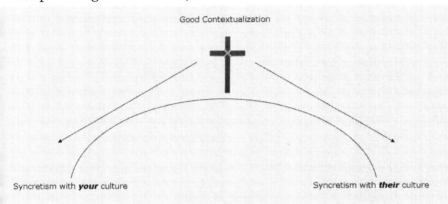

For example, one of the most frequent areas of cultural distinction that I (Seth) run into with natives of the Bronx is the role that cosmic spiritual powers are active in the lives of many of our friends. I grew up in fairly conservative Protestant churches in the Southwest. Before moving to New York City, I had never met anyone who seriously practiced astrology or believed that they could manipulate the forces of chance. Now, however, it is not unusual when I meet someone to be asked, "What is your sign?" Both astrological signs and totems of good fortune are high priorities to my newest friends. In this instance, it is not good contextualization to defer back to my culture of origin, denying that there are principalities and powers outside of those we can see which affect our lives. Despite the fact that I grew up not believing in the reality of these powers, the Gospel speaks to this issue, it is relevant to my friends, and it would damage witness to the Gospel to dismiss their beliefs as "fictions." It would do little good to attempt to challenge these beliefs or practices on the basis of my own cultural instincts. In fact, this would be syncretism with my own culture: to believe that the Gospel only speaks to what it has spoken to in our own culture. Approaching these elements through my own cultural myths would likely simply push these practices "underground" rather than allowing the Gospel to challenge and transform them.

We may be tempted to dismiss as untrue beliefs that are not native to our culture of origin; however, we must be careful not to act as if the Gospel has nothing to say to these issues. Whether they are true or not is generally not actually the issue at hand. In fact the Gospel does indeed speak to those who become preoccupied with exploring and controlling the elemental forces of the universe. Paul has strong words on this subject for both to the Galatian (Gal. 4:8–11) and Colossian churches (Col 2:8–23). To model his method of engagement is neither to deny the issue nor to supplant the values of the Gospel with the values of the culture, but rather, to contextualize.

On the other hand, a more subtle syncretism would be to present the Gospel as if it replaces these powers in giving cosmic authority to the follower of Jesus. It would be easy to pander to the desires and values of the community in a way that would lead to acceptance of a message that is not truly the Gospel. While those baptized into Christ are promised a particular kind of security, we are not given knowledge or power over the forces of the universe in a way promised by astrological practices, and we have no ability to manipulate fortune to produce better outcomes for us and for our families. To allow these values of cosmic security to supplant the values of trust and submission to the authority of God is to bypass contextualization and enter into a form of syncretism,

Another way to think about the difference between contextualization and syncretism is to use the model of "forms and substance." Contextualization takes the *forms* of culture— language, structures, concepts—and fills them with the *substance* of the Gospel. We see this in the New Testament in the parables of Jesus and even in the language of the Kingdom of God. Jesus and the evangelists use the familiar ideas of kingdom, farming, and familial relationships to communicate Gospel. The notion that God is a king (1 Samuel 8:4–9) would make little sense to people who had no experience of living in a kingdom. The idea that God is our father and Jesus is the firstborn among many siblings (Romans 8:29) is understandable in the context of a specific culture's myths about family. If, for example, Paul had come to preach among the Mosuo—an ethnic community in rural China who do not practice marriage and have no established role for paternity, a community which could rightfully be called "a society without fathers" (Stacey, 2009, p. 294)—then he would have to rely on some other explanation of God's relationship to humanity for the initial hearing the Gospel to make sense to this community.

Syncretism, on the other hand, takes the *forms* of Scripture— the same concepts the New Testament writers used to communicate the message in their own culture—and injects the *substance* of its own culture. We see this when biblical language about the Kingdom is misdirected into expressions of nationalism, or when scriptural references to the family are used to idolize the nuclear American family. We see it when the church's respect for the suffering and sacrifices of early Christians becomes worship of the Saints. Understanding the distinction between good contextualization and syncretism and navigating these boundaries in a daily life of cross-cultural evangelism is at the heart of quality mission work.

Another example requiring this kind of discernment is in the role of the law for our Muslim neighbors. While it is true that we are saved by the grace of Jesus rather than works of law, Protestant Americans are often too quick to reject any notion that the law is beneficial. We rush to deconstruct the notion of law with those who view observance of law as a matter of religious devotion. Approaches toward Muslim evangelism are widely debated within missiological circles, but we would suggest that such a deconstruction may not be the best starting point when working with our Muslim friends. To say to them, "No one can earn God's favor, and anyone who puts their faith in the works of law does not have true faith," would be to overlook a natural bridge for the Gospel in a culture where law is highly valued.

In contrast, we may find greater receptivity by beginning with a picture of Jesus as the definitive interpreter of God's laws, as we see him depicted in the Gospel of Matthew. Rather than degrading the status of the law, we can choose to engage the high view of law that already exists in a Muslim context—as it does in Scripture—and set up Jesus's status of authority in relation to the law. We might say, for example, "Followers of Jesus care deeply about following God's laws; in fact, Jesus said that he did not come to do away with the law but to fulfill it. We believe, though, that if we truly wish to understand God's purpose in giving us the law, we must understand Jesus's teachings. The one who understands Jesus comes to the fullest understanding of God's laws." This is not syncretism; it is not a twisting of the Gospel. However, it is an adaptation from the typical way we choose to understand the Gospel in our own cultural setting. While remaining faithful to Scripture, it is a contextualization towards our Muslim neighbors' respect and value for the law, which does not undermine the values of Scripture, but also does not supplant a healthy theology of grace with a works righteousness that would indeed be antithetical to the Gospel itself.

Practice

Determining My Boundaries

Each of the following is a cultural issue that may require formal or conceptual contextualization, but represents a potential misstep into syncretism. Review each of the follow and determine whether you could affirm the decision. Circle your answer in the choices below.

1. A missionary among the Inuit people adapts "lamb of God" to "baby seal of God" to preserve the metaphor in a way which may be understood.

    Good Contextualization or **Syncretism**

2. A missionary among Chinese changes the "whiteness" of Jesus's clothes in the transfiguration story to red, as white is the color of death and red the color of purity.

    Good Contextualization or **Syncretism**

3. When a missionary among Hindus notices that people place a picture of their family's god above the door of their homes, she puts a picture of Jesus above hers.

    Good Contextualization or **Syncretism**

4. A missionary notices that the primary social nexus of his community is a bar. He begins to frequent it but makes sure others are aware that he isn't drinking alcohol because he is a Christian.

    Good Contextualization or **Syncretism**

Section Two

The Gospel Engages Culture

In the following chapters, we will briefly highlight some key myths that play out in the context of different cultures. First, it is generally a helpful step to identify how these myths may or may not play out in the narratives of our own culture. This self-reflection will heighten our own sensitivity to cultural issues and sharpen our ministry skills for carrying the Gospel across cultures. Second, it will be useful to think through the ways these myths may operate in the narratives and lifestyles of the community that the church is seeking to reach.

By identifying the myths of a culture or subculture, we may recognize key elements that will need to be addressed by the Gospel. We will begin to identify the bridges that already exist for communicating the Gospel, and to understand what obstacles may inhibit a full embodiment of the good news of the Kingdom within a cultural group as well as specific barriers to our ministry or church planting strategy.

By identifying cultural myths, we are not restricted to rigid or monolithic cultural categories. Rather we inquire how each culture or subculture is interpreting or addressing different components of human experience. In global contexts, engaging cultural myths allows us to move beyond static understandings of culture and facilitate the

Mosaic

truth of the Gospel to engage pre-existing myths within each culture. It is not a matter of labeling a culture as representing or not representing a certain myth as a generalization; rather, as we engage various subcultures in a global society, in what ways do we see each of these myths playing out in each cultural setting so that we can bring them into encounter with the Gospel of Christ?

We will explore some key cultural myths—first, those we like to call "myths of empire." Myths of empire help us understand how people within a culture are interacting with stories of power, religious nationalism, and colonialism. These myths inform us as we determine how the challenges of the Gospel call us to change as Christians who come from a position of power as well as what it might require of us in pursuing justice for "the least of these." Understanding myths of empire will open the door to help us see how our citizenship is derived from the same Kingdom as that of our international Christian brothers and sisters.

Second we will look at myths of inclusion. Myths of inclusion help us to recognize the strong identification and intense loyalties that may exist within a particular group or community. These are especially prevalent in cultures with highly developed concepts of honor and shame, such as many Asian and Arab ethnic groups, but which are also easily recognizable in American gang culture. The presence of this myth has a significant impact on evangelism and church planting strategies, as we consider whether or not to embrace new frameworks for understanding or communicating sin and what is required in "one another ministry."

The third type of myth we will examine are those concerned with law. Myths about law demonstrate the importance—or lack of importance—of established institutional frameworks: laws, formal structures of authority, judicial processes, caste, etc. Understanding the place of law in a society informs the missionary of the bridges and barriers that might be present within a person's cultural understanding regarding concepts such as righteousness, authority, or morality. These myths are integral to any mission that hopes to help new Christians develop indigenous structures of leadership that are in keeping with the self-emptying character we see modeled in Jesus.

Fourth, we will turn our attention to myths about spiritual powers that highlight a culture's viewpoint when it comes to spiritual forces, fortune, or the demonic. Recognizing these myths will help us discern potential contrasts with our own cultural myths regarding spiritual powers and understand how the Gospel challenges both our own and our neighbor's understanding of and engagement with spiritual forces.

It is important to remember that the mythic framework allows us to recognize, affirm, and engage communities in which multiple myths are operating. Just because our Arab neighbor seems to prioritize inclusive myths does not mean that we should not try to bridge from his myths about spiritual powers when sharing the Gospel. Just because our Chinese friends come from a highly hierarchical culture (which is a facet of myths of law) does not mean that we should expect conflict resolution to operate under their legal myths. Typically among our Chinese friends, the inclusive values of honor and shame take precedence in conflict resolution despite the importance of legal myths.

The question, then, is not "Is this an inclusive, legal, spiritualist, or imperial culture?" Rather we must ask, which myths rule which areas of life in this community in various circumstances or contexts? When encountering culture in urban settings, multiple myths are likely in operation. Approaching cross-cultural encounters through the lens of myths allows us take a multilayered approach in communities experiencing cultural change rather than limiting our understanding to monolithic generalizations. Each culture experiences multiple myths with varying frequency and emphasis, and in diaspora communities pre-existing myths may be clashing or even mixing with newly discovered versions as cultures and subcultures interact on a daily basis. Listening for cultural myths provides a dynamic avenue for growing in our understanding of cultural expressions and recognizing bridges and barriers for the Gospel.

Fifth we will turn our attention to the interplay between myths and cultural holidays. Experiencing cultural holidays and festivals is often a way to open a window into our neighbor's culture. Quite often, holidays are like myths with a megaphone. By observing and participating in cultural festivities, cross-cultural missionaries have the opportunity to experience the culture when it is on full display. In diaspora communities undergoing cultural change, rituals and holidays provide an opportunity to observe cultural elements that are retained and elements that are abandoned and to explore the significance of these cultural adaptations for a particular culture. These are important moments for participant observation and for building relationship with our diaspora neighbors, as we, as cultural outsiders, take part in events they value.

Finally, we will look at myths about time. Realizing myths about time helps us to understand how people see themselves within the scope of history and how they see themselves in relation to the future. The Gospel is, at its heart, a historical narrative, the climax of which is rooted in the past and which claims a future culmination. Understanding differences between cyclical and linear views of time can reveal different opportunities and challenges in our Gospel proclamation. Recognizing the concern or the lack of concern for future oriented or afterlife issues will help to clarify or correct potential bridges between the culture and our presentation of the Gospel.

The chart below outlines the narrative structure of the myths being presented in the following chapters. Since myths are carriers of meaning, they are driven by an inherent desire within the culture. Each myth faces particular challenges to be realized, and each myth plays out in a particular context. As subcultures pursue the realization of a set of myths, they are embracing a set of expectations for how this myth is realized and the end result of that realization. As such, various myths provide narrative structures within a culture. As cross-cultural evangelists, we are tasked with discovering the meaning and interpretation of myths within a culture or subculture. We must discover what a Gospel encounter looks like as the narrative of Christ encounters the mythic narratives of the culture.

As we seek to communicate the Gospel across cultures, each of these cultural myths provides a framework for us to determine what aspects of a culture may be challenged by the Gospel, and what aspects might be affirmed or used to express truths of the Gospel. As we serve the mission of God within increasingly diverse cities in North America, we need dynamic frameworks for interpreting the worldviews, behaviors, traditions, and customs in relation to the good news of God's Kingdom. By discovering the underlying myths of a cultural group, we become better equipped to engage the culture as

Mosaic

ambassadors of the Gospel of Christ. By interpreting these encounters through cultural myths, we are applying a narrative approach that is simple and understandable to what may otherwise be rather complex interactions.

Story Structure of Myths

Myth	What is the primary desire?	What are the obstacles to mythic realization?	Where does realization take place?	How does realization take place?	What is the end result?
Empire	Cultural Self-Actualization	Foreign Domination and/or a Departure from Foundational Values	Political Sphere	By Obtaining the Power to Shape the Values of the State	Restoration/ Cultural Climax
Inclusion	Communal Stability	Breach of Relationship	The "Tribe"	By Honoring Correct and Shaming Incorrect Behavior	Tribal Solidarity/ Tradition
Law	Order	Unregulated Elements which Invite Chaos	The "System"	By Systematizing Relationship and Behavior	Cultural Accountability /Precedent
Spiritual Power	Harmony	Spiritual Disorder	The "Excluded Middle"	By Achieving Balance in the World of the Unseen	Dissolution of Fear

Chapter 8

Myths about Empire

The people were initially a band of disparate tribes warring with one another and with their neighbors until a ruler rose from among their ranks and unified the people to take the land in full. This ushered in a time of peace and prosperity, representing the highest point in the history of their culture. In the years since, however, the greatness of the people has diminished. The current generation must return to the values that once made them great; they must rediscover their lost identity in order to take back their cultural place of privilege. Until such a time, they hold up the memory of their kingdom's founding and hope for another leader to come and help them restore their former identity.

This, in various forms, is the myth of empire. It was the story of the Jewish people who awaited the Messiah during the second temple period in which Jesus lived. The myth of empire was at the center of the power struggles of Rome during the period of the early church. It was also the story of the Arabs at the time of the Arab revolt during the first world war, looking to both Ibn Saud and the Hashemite dynasty as the faithful successors of the Caliphate (Korda, 2010, 55–56). Listening to the members of one of our Chinese house churches explain it, this myth plays a large part in the propaganda of the Chinese government. It also seems to play a primary role in the national identities of Russia and of the United States (Khlevniuk, 2015, pp. x–xi, 7–8) both of which

151

seek to restore a more glorious era. From the authors' reading of history, the myth of empire was strong in Europe until the events of the twentieth century put a nail in the coffin of the European empires.

When Cicero sought to persuade the senate to resist the treachery of Catiline, he called them to the Temple of Jupiter which, according to tradition, had been established seven centuries earlier by Rome's founding father, Romulus. At the end of his speech to them, Cicero speaks directly to the Roman god, invoking the inheritance of city and empire he now wishes to preserve. Mary Beard (2015) argues that these appeals to Rome's origin were typical in ancient political rhetoric. She states, "The implication that Cicero was casting himself as a new Romulus was not lost on the Romans of his day . . . This was a classic Roman appeal to the founding fathers, to the stirring tales of early Rome and to the moment when the city came into being" (53–54).

It should not surprise us, then, that lionized figures in contemporary politics continue to do the same. It is no coincidence that Reagan came to office on the promise to "make America great again," which was the campaign slogan for the 1980 presidential election. This appeal to America's cultural origin is only a recycling of the imperial myth. Even in cases where a people are already in power, the desire for cultural self-actualization may still be seen in political rhetoric. As an example we can see the myth articulated in one of Napoleon's speeches to his troops preceding their campaign in Egypt. "Europe is watching you. You have a great destiny to fulfill, battles to fight, dangers and hardships to overcome. You hold in your hands the future prosperity of France, the good of mankind and your own glory. The ideal of Liberty that has made the Republic the arbiter of Europe

will also make it the arbiter of distant oceans, of faraway countries...."
(Roberts, 2014, p. 165).

We see the myth of empire at any time that the party coming into power identifies itself as the continuation or renewal of the foundational ideals of the particular culture or people. It may arise whenever a debate occurs between two parties as to which of the powers were foundational to the culture: e.g. the tension between China's identification with Mao's Cultural Revolution or the traditional Chinese culture Mao tried to destroy, or the Marxist subversion of the Latin American puppet states in the name of the populist powers which existed before. The myth of empire is lived out and recycled again and again among the nations. It is one of the central myths the Gospel directly addresses. The Gospel that Jesus proclaimed in his first century world stood in stark contrast to the myths of empire—Jewish and Roman alike—and the Gospel remains a challenge to our contemporary myths which persistently compete with the Kingdom of God for our absolute allegiance.

The Imperial Myths of the Oppressed

On the other side of these narratives we might look at those peoples who live on the receiving end of an enduring history of colonialism: For centuries, the Latin American peoples and African nations have been pawns of those who uphold the myth of empire and perhaps no people have had a more tangled experience of empire than those of the Indian subcontinent. Beginning with the colonialism of Europe but evolving through the industrial revolution and current structures of global production and trade, the majority world also is heavily invested in the myth of empire as well, only from the position of the ruled and dominated.

To understand fully the myth of empire it is helpful to understand the Marxist myth, which has had great influence in the former colonial states. Marxism is not an alternative to the imperial myth, but a variation of the same story: the rise of the common people will bring about the climax of history and restoration of culture, and the redistribution of the forces of labor will serve the messianic function of a returned great king or leader (Marx & Engels, 2008, pp. 6–8). The imperial myth, in all of its forms does not require any position of power to maintain itself. Rather, is it is a cultural narrative that plays out in our aspirations, fears, and behaviors. Both the powerful and the oppressed reach for the hopes and longings inherent within this myth. We can detect this myth playing out among those with whom we minister, and we can see it within ourselves as well, competing for our allegiance to the Kingdom of God.

Those who have power use the myth of empire to consolidate and propagate their identity into the next generation; but when we look at the use of this myth by the Arab peoples of the early twentieth century, the Indian subcontinent, and the Jews of the first century, we see a people who are under the power of the empires of their day. This position of domination does not prevent them from viewing themselves through the myth of empire. Rather, they live with the expectation and hope that their empire will rise and replace the present one. This was the question and expectation that Jesus's disciples kept repeating to him in anticipation of a restored empire displacing their oppressors despite Jesus's alternative vision of Kingdom. The powerless and the marginalized can live within and work out the imperial myth while they await its actualization in the coming age.

An important principle when identifying the potential myths of empire that might exist among a diaspora community is to keep the Gospel of God's Kingdom at the center of our message and of any ministry aspirations. The myth of empire highlights how important it is that we recognize the power dynamics of culture at work. It is central to the message of the Gospel that we call people to place their hope in Jesus as Lord, rather than simply shifting their allegiance from the culture of one worldly empire to that of another. Becoming sensitive to the myth of empire increases our ability to maintain a faithful witness for the Gospel of Christ as we wade through the sea of cultures, tribes, and languages mingling—and sometimes conflicting—in our cities.

Preaching the Kingdom of God

In the Gospels, we see the oppositional beliefs Jesus confronts in trying to prevent his message about God's coming kingdom from being co-opted by the myth of empire:

Pilate went back into the palace. He summoned Jesus and asked, "Are you the king of the Jews?" Jesus answered, "Do you say this on your own or have others spoken to you about me?" Pilate responded, "I'm not a Jew, am I? Your nation and its chief priests handed you over to me. What have you done?" Jesus replied, "My kingdom doesn't originate from this world. If it did, my guards would fight so that I wouldn't have been arrested by the Jewish leaders. My kingdom isn't from here." "So you are a king?" Pilate said. Jesus answered, "You say that I am a king. I was born and came into the world for this reason:

to testify to the truth. Whoever accepts the truth listens to my voice." (John 18:33–37)

Jesus's listeners were not seeking to make him their king by force so that he could become the enemy-loving Prince of Peace. To them, he was the answer to their longings for a restored and glorious empire. Even in Acts 1, following the resurrection, his disciples ask, "Lord, is this the time when you will restore the kingdom to Israel?" Minutes before the ascension they are still expecting their own myth of empire to finally be fulfilled. And his disciples are not alone in their syncretism. In interpreting the Scriptures, it may be important to question whether we are reading with the original message in mind or through our own contemporary assumptions about empire. In European history we can see that time and again the myth of empire has subsumed the notion of God's kingdom and that the church has acted as a tool for the advancement of political power and a national agenda (e.g., the Crusades or the religious wars of the Reformation.)

This is not an issue that only exists in the past, however. We should be prepared to engage the myth of empire in any variety of forms among our diaspora neighbors. In working with our South Asian neighbors, for example, our team must be cautious when offering services to the community. We fear that in their cultural context, people may pretend to be interested in the Gospel in order to gain the status or privileges they associate with our identity as Americans. We truly desire to serve the community, but as citizens of the host nation, we do not want the Gospel to be seen as a gateway to imperial privilege or a ladder to power. We also must be careful when using the language of Kingdom, because it may sound as if we, as citizens of a country which has a history of coercive economic relationship with their nation of origin, are offering them the chance to become like us as Americans rather than to shift their allegiance from one culture or nation over to an allegiance to Jesus as the true King of Kings. The Kingdom of God regularly confronts each of our myths of empire in its various forms.

I (Jared) was meeting with a Mexican brother in the Lord for several months. During this time, he invited a friend of his from Guatemala to join us for a Bible discussion in his neighborhood. Several months passed and his friend still did not join our meeting. Finally, one day I walked into the McDonald's where we met, and he and his Guatemalan friend were waiting for me to arrive. He was obviously happy to meet me, and as the conversation progressed into the evening, he declared that if he had just known that his Mexican friend was meeting with an Anglo, he would have come a long time ago. As a Central American immigrant to the United States, he openly acknowledged the perceived advantages of connecting with one possessing higher social status in the dominant culture. While indeed some will respond to members of the dominant culture with animosity, many others will view us as representing higher status simply because we were born with a certain demographic profile. However, as Jesus commanded, the Gospel calls us into a mutual fellowship where one does not lord over the other, especially in reference to worldly position or status (Mark 10:35–45). The Gospel of the Kingdom undermines systems of caste and class for the sake of the beloved community.

The myth of empire can subtly undermine the efforts of the Gospel of God's Kingdom. Being aware of these nuanced concerns can help cross-cultural ambassadors of Christ keep the message of the Gospel central. Our social status, rooted as it is in the myth of empire, is an ever-present reality for American Christians working among different cultures. Therefore, a deep and self-critical understanding of our imperial myths is critical for healthy mission. Remaining sensitive to the workings of the myth of empire both within ourselves and among those we are serving will help us maintain the Gospel of God's Kingdom as our central focus.

In summary, the imperial myth plays out in a myriad of ways in every society. For some, the myth of empire manifests itself in their aspirations. It remains as a hope on the horizon. For others, this myth is realized in a desire to maintain their existing position. We must be shrewd in our effort to leave the Gospel free to subvert the myths of empire that exist both in our own culture and in the cultures of those we wish to reach.

Practice One

Identify ways that the myth of empire might have played out in your own experiences. How does the myth of empire affect your culture or subculture? Does it impact the way you interpret Scripture or give weight to different concepts? Are there things that you might say or do differently in ministry relationships in order to avoid transmitting assumptions about empire rather than the Gospel of Christ? List any reflections that come to mind.

Notes:

Practice Two

In reflecting on your diaspora neighbor's culture, identify its relationship to the imperial myth and the effect this might have on your presentation of the Gospel. How does the Gospel challenge their version of the myth of empire? How might this myth affect the interactions between your cultures? Reflect on the historical relationship of your neighbor's culture to your own, and the way that this might affect the community's perception of you as an outsider. Keep in mind there may be different responses among different subcultures within the wider diaspora community. Consider what stories in Scripture might directly challenge their notions of the power structures of this world. Make a list of these Scriptures and reflect on the ways they challenge the existing myths in the culture.

Notes:

Practice Three

Bible Story Sets

You have a group of African immigrants ready to gather for a Bible study. You want to develop a list of passages from Scripture to serve as a series for their weekly study. Their level of literacy is low, so you will have to relate the Bible stories orally to the leader who interpret them into the tribal language for the rest of the group. You cannot predict how many of the details will be retained as the story is retold. For your contacts, agreeing to this Bible study may be a way of improving their relationship with an American so that you may provide favors for members who attend.

Develop a set of six Bible stories you will cover in the study that might engage and challenge the way the myth of empire is at play in this context. Keep in mind that you want the group to come to these conclusions on their own primarily through discussion rather than through your teaching, in order not to reinforce your role as the one with power in the relationship. You want to gather them around the Scriptures so that they, as cultural insiders, may begin to contextualize the stories within their own cultural group. Ideally, they will begin to discover the viewpoint of the Scriptures rather than any potential assumptions regarding social status. This requires that the stories challenge the myth of empire overtly, rather than relying on a heavy exegesis or expository teaching in order to understand how the myth is relevant. When selecting stories, try to include the passion and resurrection as a topic for one of the weeks.

List the story set below and discuss how the death and resurrection of Jesus might be understood as challenging to the myth of empire.

Mosaic

Notes:

Chapter 9

Myths about Inclusion

In order to survive the inhospitable world, there is no value higher than your membership in the group. There is no identity more central than your position in the community. You do not have much value or status apart from the tribe, and the tribe's value is contingent on its standing in relationship to the groups which view it from the outside. This makes harmony with others the highest priority and bringing shame on the community the greatest sin. No pursuit is more worthy than bringing honor to the group, and a member who brings shame on the group must be excluded or even killed in order to save the reputation of the whole. An individual who gains status raises the status of the tribe and a member who loses face lowers the status of the tribe. Any member must be willing to sacrifice themselves in order to uphold the honor of the whole body and help preserve face.

This is the myth of inclusion. Whether it concerns the household, the tribe, the race, or the nation, the myth of inclusion constructs a corporate identity that must be preserved and passed on to the next generation. While it exists in every culture, the myth of inclusion is most visible in societies which possess strong concepts of honor and shame: that is to say, cultures that appeal to one's relationship to the community as more authoritative when assigning

163

blame and understanding right behavior than one's relationship to the law or to the spirit world. These honor-shame oriented cultures tend to be more common in the majority world, including Islamic cultures.

We might understand the myth of inclusion in our context through the life of my (Seth's) friend Antonio. Growing up in the South Bronx, many of Antonio's earliest memories are of shoot-outs and police raids. Around age thirteen, Antonio and his cousins began selling drugs on the street corners and were frequently in and out of jail. Dealing drugs, however, was seen as a savvy and even noble vocation because of the amount of money one could make for oneself and one's family. The higher Antonio ascended the ladder of the trade, the greater his reputation and the more status he brought to his neighborhood. As their status increased though, his friends on the block began to challenge rival gangs on the next block. These rivalries could only be settled through street-fights to establish who actually had the honor of representing the neighborhood as the true gang from their region. To lose territory (in this case meaning street corners to sell on) or to have one's graffiti tags covered over by the rival gangs was the ultimate act of shame. A member of the neighborhood who could not adequately stand up for their block was seen as too weak to be an acknowledged part of the community. The members of the neighborhood would be slow to claim the offender, if they acknowledge them at all, as a part of the community.

After leaving the gangbanger life behind, Antonio found a job at an auto shop where he was frequently cheated out of his wages and verbally abused by his manager. Rather than leave and find better employment, Antonio stayed for several more years, even turning down jobs that paid twice as much. He chose to live in substandard housing and let his family go on welfare rather than leave because leaving would show his boss and the neighborhood that Antonio was not tough enough to withstand the abuse. Quitting would establish his reputation as being less of a man than his boss. Instead of leaving, he remained until the boss died. Having established his reputation he then left and found better work.

When I speak with Antonio and his extended family, there is no sense that their past behavior was wrong simply because it was illegal or criminal. The rightness of their actions is all determined in relationship to how it affected the status of the group—both the family and the neighborhood. In their perspective, Antonio and his friends were at their best in life when they were bringing cash and reputation to the neighborhood. Now that they are too old to be gangbangers, they actually live at a much higher economic level and are in line with the law, yet they see their new jobs and lives as a step down because they are no longer able to maintain the fierce reputation they saw as essential to their livelihood. Antonio's story is one best understood through the myth of inclusion.

We see a larger expression of the myth of inclusion in Christopher Clark's discussion of the Balkans in the years leading up to the first world war. In his words:

> When the Carnegie Foundation dispatched a commission to the area to investigate atrocities committed in the course of the Second Balkan War, they found it impossible to establish a local consensus on the ethnicity of the people living in Macedonia, so polarized was the atmosphere in which these issues were discussed, even at the universities. The report the commission published in that year included not one, but two ethnic maps of the region, reflecting the view from Belgrade and the view from Sofia respectively. In one, western and northern Macedonia pullulate with unliberated Serbs awaiting unification with their

motherland, in the other, the region appeared as the heartland of the Bulgarian zone of settlement. During the last decades of the nineteenth century, the Serbs, the Greeks and the Bulgarians all ran highly active propaganda agencies inside Macedonia whose purpose was to proselytize the local Slavs to their respective national causes (Clark, 2013, p. 25).

Notice how different the notion of ethnicity becomes when it is defined, not by some official legal structure, established national borders, or institutionalized "races," but by belonging to a particular community. The boundaries of nation-states did not determine one's identity, but instead identity was rooted in "tribe" or people in a way that paid little attention to legal boundaries. In this example, there is a clear difference between the myth of law (which we will discuss in the following chapter) and the myth of inclusion in understanding ethnic identity. Groups formed around identities forged through cultural myths rather than borders imposed by legal powers.

In the life of the church, we see the myth of inclusion in those traditions which practice excommunication or "disfellowshipping" as a primary means of ecclesiastic discipline. However, it may do little good to exclude one from the community where the myth of inclusion carries little weight. In a more legalized community, we could expect church discipline to take the form of a systematized set of disciplines corresponding to specific behaviors and a primary punishment would be stripping an individual of an office or issuing a hierarchical demotion. Communal exclusion and its accompanying fear in the life of a believer could only function where inclusion was a primary myth. It is telling of the enormous cultural reach of the Catholic church that we see both inclusive and legal myths operating with nearly equal authority in their structure of church discipline.

Often, our presentations of the Gospel are centered on the individual and rooted in a sense of personal guilt. This is an effective way to communicate the Gospel when the hearers function and understand their relationship to the world around them in a similar manner (i.e., in cultures with well established legal myths) and where individual lawfulness or guilt are central themes. However, in many cultures the myth of inclusion is of central importance. Their standing is in relation to their place in the group. Rather than function within a framework of systematized statuses of right or wrong, they might think in terms of honor or shame (Kraft, 2008, pp. 179–182). We do not have to look far in Scripture to begin understanding how to interact as ambassadors of the Gospel with such cultural assumptions: the myth of inclusion is one of the primary operating myths in the cultural world of the Bible.

The myth of inclusion has its fingerprints all over the Christian Scriptures, tying strongly into the theological language of adoption, identity as a people, or the sanctity of the name—particularly God's name. You might think of how often in Scripture sin causes God to turn his face from the people, or how often a righteous person lifts up God's name among the nations. Or we might consider Paul's theology of the Gentiles as being adopted into the family of God through Christ's resurrection (Eph.2:11–22). When all have sinned and fall short of the glory of God, it is not so much a legal problem that requires adjudication, but a restoration of honor to those who are trapped in shame. How can we understand the drama of the prodigal son outside of the inclusive myth? Or what would we understand about Yom Kippur? In Leviticus, the Day of Atonement requires a ceremony in which the sin (singular) of the people is placed upon a scapegoat—

which is not sacrificed but is expelled from among the people—so that the sin might be removed from the group and they can remain in harmonic relationship with God. This is atonement as understood through the myth of inclusion.

On his deathbed, one of our friend Napdeth's final actions as head of his household was to tell his brother and son to let two of the cousins back into the family. In the past these cousins had dishonored the family and were expelled from the group; now that Napdeth was dying, he felt that it was time to offer conciliation and open the door for them to be restored. However, in the event that the cousins would not admit their shame and re-enter humbly, he told his family to rescind the offer of their being adopted back in. This is what reconciliation looks like in an inclusive South Asian culture. The Gospel is deeply concerned with understanding God's mission through this lens.

For many of us from highly individualistic cultures in the United States, it may be difficult to grasp the power of inclusion in other cultures. However, not only do we find this myth at work in the cultural world of our Bibles, but the myth of inclusion may play a prominent role when addressing issues of conversion, church conflict, and a number of other themes that come up in ministry. It will be important for American Christians to look beyond our strong inclination towards individualism in order to understand the dilemma facing other cultures with whom we may be serving.

Practice One

Case Study

You have helped plant a Korean speaking church in your neighborhood, and one of your leaders is moving back to Seoul where he plans to plant a new house church. While this leader grew up in Seoul and recognizes that there are numerous healthy churches in the area, he wants to work with young professionals in his relational network who—as has also happened frequently in the United States— have either left church in their teenage years or are only nominally involved now that they are adults. He wants to utilize these friendships to restore discipleship among his peers and see a growth of the Gospel among those who have ceased being a part of an established Korean church. He has no ill-will towards the existing churches and sees them as partners in ministry, not competitors. He simply hopes to begin a house church that will provide an expression of church that his peers might find approachable for returning to faith.

However, a small group of church leaders in his home community back in Korea are skeptical about his approach to ministry and think that his emphasis on small group ministry is likely to undermine the authority of the established churches there. They say that if he wants to be involved in ministry then he should be encouraging his friends to attend services at an established congregation because this is what is required of a faithful Christian. Of course, he realizes that his friends have already given up on church. Simply inviting them back to churches that they have intentionally left is not a likely solution. Your Korean friend calls you and explains the situation. He knows that if he does what is asked of him by these

Christian leaders then his work among his peer group will be ineffective because his peers have already experienced this expression of faith and have already rejected it. However, he is afraid that if he does not do as they ask then any new house churches he starts will begin with a shameful reputation in the community and will be unable to change that perception afterwards. He finds himself stuck between an effective ministry strategy among his peers on the one hand and his potential standing in his community on the other. What do you advise him to do? Explain how the myth of inclusion is at play here.

Notes:

Practice Two

Case Study

You work among the Kosovar Albanian diaspora that has formed an ethnic enclave in your city. You have encountered few people with a stronger ethnic or tribal identity than your friends, as they view themselves by their national or ethnic identity first and anything else a distant second. In speaking with them you come to understand that, while this same corporate identity is primary among Albanians overseas, cognitive dissonance may be at play in the diaspora community to intensify the myth of inclusion. An integral part of this ethnic identity is the Kosovar Albanian history with other Eastern European ethnic groups: your friends share an overwhelmingly negative history with both Serbians and Russians who now live the same area of the city. Their small nation was among the Eastern European communist states and went through violent conflict with the Serbians following the end of the Cold War. Their history with the Soviet Union and a violent past with Serbia places a natural animosity between them and their neighbors who have arrived in your community from these other nations. Often these immigrant groups settle into the same neighborhoods in the city, but ethnic tensions remain high even if under the surface.

Because you believe that loving enemies is central to maturing as the people of God, you think it is imperative to share this as a part of your Gospel presentation. However, it has been extraordinarily difficult for you to form friendships in this community because you are not a cultural insider, and you know that you would destroy the limited inclusion you have been granted by shaming your friends through verbalizing the implication that the centrality of their ethnic identity is at odds with obeying God. While the Gospel indeed challenges every culture, you are still building bridges and working to gain traction in this community. The gains you have made into this diaspora community over many months have been difficult to say the least. You do not desire to lose the relational progress that has been made; however, you do desire to allow the Gospel to speak directly into their community. What do you do? How is the myth of inclusion at work here?

Notes:

Practice Three

Case Study

You find a Muslim friend who is receptive to your message about Jesus, but she is afraid to respond in any publicly visible way because she believes that it will bring shame on her family for her to leave Islam behind. If it were only a matter of her own reputation, she might be willing to come out openly; but she cannot bear to damage the reputation of her father's household in the eyes of the community by openly shaming them in becoming a Christian. What do you advise her to do? How does the potential strain between her and her Muslim community impact your strategy for sharing the Gospel in this community? As this is your first potential convert from this Muslim community, what alternative community do you offer in order to help her fulfill her cultural need for the myth of inclusion to be expressed?

Notes:

Practice Four

Case Study

Your friend Khan is the owner of the most successful business in a South Asian community. He employs many in the neighborhood and rents property to several of the other key families: Khan is obviously one of the central gatekeepers of this diaspora neighborhood. One day when speaking with him about his children's schooling, Khan tells you an interesting story. "I do not worry about my children learning the wrong values from their American teachers," he says. "If they come home and tell me something that they have been taught which I know is wrong, I simply say to them, 'Yes, your teacher is very wise, but let me add something to what she has said.' This way they know what is right, but they still can honor their teacher."

What does Khan's story teach you about the role of the myth of inclusion in this community? How does this affect how you evaluate the responses to your own message within this community? How does this affect how you respond in apologetic conversations, when a Muslim teacher attempts to convince you of spiritual truth from an Islamic point of view? What does this teach you about how differences of opinion are handled in important relationships?

Notes:

Chapter 10

Myths about the Law

No person is above the law. Whether it is the legislative body that arises from the social contract or the rule of life given to humanity by God. The law governs, guides, protects, and preserves us as a people. The law allows others to be integrated into our community, it serves to initiate us all into the larger society and guards us against the tyranny and caprice of those who would seek to obtain power. Without the law, all of society would collapse and anarchy would consume the community. Without the law, there would be no future for our society, there would be no security for our culture. Without the law, we would have no stable foundation upon which to understand our identity or how we should relate to one another.

This is the myth of law. Cultures that value the myth of law tend to organize, stratify, classify, and create hierarchies and structures to understand and govern relationship. Although it is unique to each culture where the authority to create or transform law is located, law frequently operates within the same narratives and creates similar issues when engaging the Gospel. Although the myth of law exists in most cultures, it is most visible in those cultures with highly developed notions of guilt and innocence: that is to say those cultures who tend to appeal to the law as more authoritative than one's relationship to the tribe or the spirit world when assigning blame and understanding right behavior.

We see myths about law in almost every culture and they affect many different facets of everyday life. Nicky Gumble once shared an illustration about a group of kids on a soccer field. No coach or teacher was yet present, so the kids were just running chaotically across the field with no real order to their spontaneous release of human energy. Some kids were left out while others monopolized the ball. Still others found themselves frustrated by the apparent anarchy. You would think that such an unrestricted and unguided event would be fun, but unbridled anarchy is not a fun way to play soccer. When someone stepped onto the field and organized the game, the children were able to flourish within the confines of the rules, expectations, and morals of the game of soccer. In examples such as this, it is obvious how the role of the "law" is presented as helpful and necessary in our lives. Laws give us an understanding of how to live and arrange our relationships with one another. The law brings order and structure out of a chaotic network of actions and relationships. It allows us to integrate and regulate new experiences into a known world.

The myth of the law has its fingerprints all over the Scriptures, first (obviously) in the Jewish law, but arising again as a primary myth in Paul's dealings with the Gentile cultures that strongly identified with Roman social order. We see in Paul's work a contextualization of the two dominate legal manifestations of his context: *Torah* and *Oikos*, Jewish Law and the Roman Family Code. The degree to which law determines identity is a major issue in Galatians and the letter to the Romans. The whole notion of covenant is colored by a myth of systematized behavior and relational transaction. And it should not be overlooked that a major theme of Jesus's teaching is the deconstruction of law's implementation as a means of creating hierarchies of personal value and achieving relational status before God. In the Sermon on the Mount we see the definitive interpreter of Torah: Jesus as the new Moses who is instructing us in the proper understanding of this law which will not pass away until everything is accomplished. The Gospel holds a paradoxical relationship to the law. It is both a fulfillment of the law (Mt. 5:17–20), a new law (covenant) written on our hearts (Heb. 9:11–22), and it teaches us that those outside law are equally loved and accepted by God (Rom. 5:6–11).

Although primarily culturally defined by the myths of inclusion and spiritual power, the law plays a special role in the form of *sharia* among Muslim people groups. In this context the law is a created structure to help one live rightly before God. Even though the formation of the legal code took the first couple of centuries to develop, the movement towards law was a primary component of Islam since its beginning (Denny, 1994, pp. 195–200). However, the cultures of Western Europe and North America especially tend to place the myth of law as a central priority in their self-understanding. Violation of the law, in these cultures, is more serious than violation of communal solidarity. One's rightness is measured by the standards of the law rather than the wellbeing or honor of the community. Unlike the myth of inclusion, a culture which prioritizes the myth of law would not view a person as justified in breaking (or not keeping) the law out of fear of violating communal relationship, and acceptance back into the community would not be enough to remove one's guilt—only justice which arises from the legal structure can declare a person guilty or innocent.

Apart from spheres of guilt and innocence, the myth of law tends to specialize in the creation of offices and hierarchies and in institutionalizing identities. This may be seen in the development of social classes in European society and in the system of caste that dominates South Asian cultures. Another area in which we might see the divergence of the inclusive and legal myths is in the rise of the sciences in 19th century Europe, particularly as they relate to the study of sexuality and of mental health. The creation of standards for what constitutes normative social and mental health is an expansion and adaptation of the legal myths: the effort of these being to create structures of systemized behavior and external standards by which to regulate society. Compare this to more inclusive cultures where social deviance is judged on the basis of the relationship one has to the community. In the legal context, one is in the wrong because one is abnormal; whether or not an abnormal person is in right relationship with the tribe is beside the point. In the creation of the behavioral sciences, violation of "the norm" became grounds for legal action, leading to the forced internment and study of those deemed deviant or abnormal (Foucault, 1978). This is why behavioral sciences evolve along with changes in societal norms and legal standards.

Another instance of legal developments may be seen in the creation of caste and classes within society. In the case of classism, these identities reveal a blending of both legal and inclusive structures. Class/Caste is a legal myth in so far as it has been institutionalized and may be identified and addressed outside of any specific relationships between individuals. We might take for instance the formalized spectrum of caste present in Indian society, or the stratification of South African society into blacks, coloreds, and whites. These designations, although socially constructed, have been codified to the extent that they exist more in the myth of law than inclusion: They are not simply values maintained by "in group" boundaries (as we would expect to find expressed in a purely inclusive myth), but have been institutionalized into formal structures. Legal myths have been created when values within a culture have been externalized into systems. In other words, legal myths are generally enforced by external pressure while inclusive myths are enforced from within the group. However, we should expect to see some overlapping or combination of these myths at work in various cultures. For our diaspora neighbors, they may come from a culture in which identities, such as caste or race, were legalized. Often, despite now living in a new context in which the formal structure no longer carries any weight, these values may continue to play out socially through myths of inclusion. For example, in the Dominican Republic Raphael Trujillo is known for leading a brutal regime that championed racist policies of "Antihatianismo." Although the racist divisions in the Dominican Republic originate in Spanish colonialism, Trujillo helped to institutionalize these attitudes (Sagás). For our purposes, we might say that his regime legalized the existing values of the culture. As the Dominican diaspora is one of the largest communities in New York City, I (Jared) spent much of my early ministry time doing ethnographic work among this community. One of the stunning things that my neighbors shared with me was the residual effects of the Trujillo government's attempt to "whiten" Dominican culture, despite the overturning of many of the formal systems. Even when any legal frameworks are removed—especially among diaspora communities now living in the United States—it is still possible to witness the influence of the legal myths present in our neighbor's culture of origin (such as classism) that persist through informal social pressures of inclusion. In a diaspora community, where previous legal structures no longer exist, myths of inclusion may still manifest previous codes as cultural norms.

Unlike the designation of authority in inclusively centered cultures, legalistic cultures tend to view authority as a matter of qualification on the basis of training, position, status, ordination, election, or certification. Authority is granted by the structure or system, and authority figures are expected to uphold and follow the code of behavior. Legal myths create a structure of authority and morality existing outside of the identity of any person within the structure. Though technically the mechanisms of power are still in the hands of the community, in the legal myth groups give their power to the created system in order to ensure social stability.

Earlier we used an example of disagreement between three new church leaders: an ex-Catholic, seeing leadership as a matter of ordination; a second young man seeing leadership as an inherited office, and me (Seth) believing it to be a matter of experience and training. All three are grounded in the myth of law, they represent differing interpretations of "right" social regulation but they emerge from the same mythic desires. The myth of law is present in the cultural background of each individual, but the ways our legal myths grapple with reality vary.

To see the difference in authority between the myth of inclusion and the myth of law, consider the following example. I (Seth) was speaking with a missionary who was visiting the Bronx to observe our work. We began to discuss one of the church groups we had planted the previous year. The group began as a house church of four individuals and as of this writing has multiplied into five groups numbering about 25 people. I shared my excitement about the new growth over the previous twelve months, especially as none of the new people know that I am a minister or that I started the group. Several of the groups do not even know me at all. The leadership of the new groups and the evangelism that brought them into these house churches took place entirely through the original members of the first church group that I began.

My friend was unimpressed, however. He said, "So when do you tell them that you are a pastor?" I told him that I do not tell them. "Well who do you tell and when?" he asked. I told him that sometimes if I am out in a restaurant or pub and the subject of what I do for work comes up, if it is an Irish or Latino crowd I may tell them I am a minister. Otherwise I like to keep that quiet until I know them better. "But would your words not carry more authority once they know that you are a minister?" my friend asked. "Wouldn't it be more effective in changing the relational dynamic towards spiritual things?" At this point I began to understand our disagreement. My friend is a savvy and gifted minister, but because we are in an American context, when he thinks of authority, he sees the myth of law as more central than the myth of inclusion.

So I explained my reasoning like this: if I began spiritual conversations with post-Christian friends by saying I was a pastor, they would immediately start adapting their behavior around that fact— either positively or negatively—because in their minds there is an institutional authority that comes with being professional clergy. This

Mosaic

is an authority created by the myth of law. However, in the long term, this institutional authority would prevent me from establishing intimate relationship with many of them, as the position of power also brings with it a hierarchy of relationship. For my post-Christian or secular friends, the same title that gives me institutional authority actually creates institutional distance. It is better for me, then, to enter through the myth of inclusion. If I develop a relational authority before there is any position between us, then although my words and actions will be less efficient when administrative issues arise, I will have access to a totally different part of their lives in the discipleship process. Further, I am modeling the type of authority that they will have access to as they move from being disciples to disciple-makers through their relationships with friends and family since they will not have positional authority as they do so. The question, then, is not whether or not I will have authority in my ministry, but what kind of authority—legal or inclusive (or as we will see in the next chapter, charismatic)—is most advantageous to the ministry I am pursuing in this context.

Practice One

Case Study

An individual who has been leading a Korean small group is about to move back to Seoul, so you have been trying to pass off leadership of the Bible study to another member of the group. Even though the group discusses a set of questions every week in church, at no point has anyone leading the group ever been expected to generate their own lesson plans or content. This new leader, at first, protests that she does not know enough to lead a Bible study. When questioned, she explains that in her early experiences of church she saw leadership limited to those who had formal education and ordination for ministry. She believes that these certifications may be necessary to facilitate a Bible study. Identify the ways in which the myth of law is operating here and how you might challenge or encourage this new leader.

Notes:

Practice Two

Case Study

You have been spending some time at a local pub, and have determined that one of the primary manifestations of brokenness in this community is unreconciled relationships—particularly in the household. Nearly everyone you meet has a network of relationships that have imploded and left anger and resentment in their wake. You have begun to share with one of your friends Jesus's teaching that reconciliation with a brother or sister is a more primary act of worship than ritual religious observance (Matt. 5). While the notion that God's primary concern is not with correct forms of worship strikes a chord in this non-religious context, his response to the notion of reconciliation is not so positive: "There is no way I could forgive my family. If you move against me once, you are done. I only talk to my mother and one of my brothers. I don't need anybody else." A few months later this friend gets in an argument with another regular at the pub and never returns. While you suspect that these actions are related to the strong myths about personal reputation in this part of the city (which is a manifestation of the myth of inclusion), you also see that solidarity with the community is not a value for individuals in this subculture. Acting in accordance with one's conscience is more primary than harmony with the group.

What challenges does this subculture present to the realization of the Gospel in this community? How might you adapt your presentation accordingly? Individuals in this culture not only devalue solidarity with the group but also believe that it is immoral to try to "guilt" individuals into right behavior. With this in mind, what is the most effective presentation of reconciliation that you can share without discrediting yourself as a messenger? Identify where the myth of law may be an obstacle in this context.

Notes:

Practice Three

Case Study

One of your most effective house church leaders grew up Catholic but drifted away as a young adult. He has come back to faith in the last few months and has since helped you plant several new churches among his network of relationships. Although he helps coach the leaders of several of these other groups and leads one of the churches himself, he continues to speak about the future when he might go to seminary and then become "a real pastor." You ask him how that would make his ministry different from what he does now. He does not have any concrete answer but continues to speak of his future plans in these terms.

Identify the way that the myth of law is at work in this relationship and how you might handle the situation. How might this affect the way that you appeal to your own education and training when explaining or coaching church leaders in this culture?

Notes:

Practice Four

You have been studying the Gospel for some time with a group of Chinese international students. It is obvious that they are from elite families and there appears to be a great disconnect between their life experiences and that of the less economically advantaged Chinese immigrant community in your city. While the myth of inclusion is primary in the social discipline of Chinese culture, you know that the legal myth dominates the way leadership functions in their home context. In fact, your friends have remarked that one of the most striking features of American culture is how familiar workers and students are with their bosses and teachers. "We would never be so informal with an authority figure in China," they have told you, "It does not show the proper respect." You have noticed in the last several months that your friends are eager to share their faith but they only do so with peers of their own social class.

Although you wish to be contextually sensitive when forming leaders for this young church, you also want to emphasize the Gospel's work in breaking down social classes as relates to systems of value before God. Jesus seemed especially concerned about including the marginalized and the economically disadvantaged, and social status did not seem to dictate one's fitness for leadership in the early church. How can you begin to engage this issue with your Chinese friends? Reflect on how you can begin planting seeds now that will grow to include the other Chinese community. One critical thing to remember is the way in which you model authority and leadership when pastoring your international students. In reaching others, if they do not reproduce their own culture they are likely to reproduce whatever they see modeled in you. How can you model a form of Christian leadership that subverts rather than reinforces a strong hierarchy in discipling relationships while remaining sensitive to their unique cultural background? As a part of your reflection, choose a story you might read for a Bible study with your neighbor and write four discussion questions that bring out implications of the story for their situation

Notes:

Chapter 11

Myths about Spiritual Power

Behind the actions we take and the experiences we have every day lays a network of spiritual powers and demonic entities. It is possible through forms of appeasement or ritual to manipulate the spiritual world, but there is always a danger that some stronger power is working against the authority you are connected with. A major part of the human condition concerns our vulnerability to these powers. One of the most basic and appropriate human emotions is fear: fear of the powers failing you, fear that envy or relational strife might induce someone to enlist the powers against you, fear that you might be cut off from the powers. Living a successful life, then, requires either an understanding of the spiritual landscape or access to the services of someone who does.

This is the myth of spiritual power. Under the myth of spiritual power, breaking the law or breaking a relationship in a way that brings shame is as taboo because of how it affects one's status in the spiritual realm. In this myth, an individual opening a new business might seek the counsel of a shaman or give gifts to a priest who has access to a certain god or saint; a mother who wishes to guarantee health for her young son might buy him an amulet; a person suffering illness or financial difficulty might seek to discern who placed a curse upon them. The spiritual world is the authority through which we interpret our experiences and the source of power to control our world (Kraft, 2008, pp. 192–196).

Near my house (Seth) is a Catholic cathedral. Inside the courtyard is a grotto where one can place a candle to aid the prayers of the petitioner and collect holy water that cascades down the inside wall like a waterfall. Often, as I walk past this religious site, there is a line of people waiting to place money in the grotto and to collect some of the water. They have come to petition the saints to advocate for them before God. This is a vivid example of the myth of spiritual power.

Some time ago, I (Jared) was meeting with a friend, a refugee from West Africa, in his New York City neighborhood. We were discussing life and ministry, and he began to share that he was facing some challenges in his marriage. Normally, as a Western minister, I begin digging for the source of the problem in some behavior, unresolved history, or feelings of neglect in the relationship. His perspective was somewhat different from mine: he explained that they were struggling against a curse from their enemies. For my African friend, a spiritual conflict was producing a crisis within human experience, and his primary response was a call to prayer.

This myth is well illustrated in the life of my friend Isabella. Several months ago Isabella asked me (Seth) to facilitate the funeral for her mother. It turned out that by funeral, she actually meant that she would like me to attend an eight-hour barbeque where the family would share stories and honor their deceased matriarch. In their stories, over and over again I heard how religious their mother had been and how frequently she had gone to the church to say prayers. Knowing that Isabella thinks quite little of religion, I was surprised to hear this about her mother. "Oh, yes," she told me, "*mami* even left me her special book of prayers." It was then that I began to suspect that we were talking about different things. I took Isabella's brother to the side and asked him, "Is your mother's book a *libreta?*" This is a book of spells used in the practice of the Caribbean religion Santeria. "Oh, yes!" he replied, "Whenever the family has a problem, mami would find the right prayer and would light a candle and use some chicken blood to see what was causing the problem. As children we often would walk through the house backwards kicking a coconut along the walls to rid the house of evil spirits."

When I asked him how it is that the family can practice these things but hate religion he explained: "This is old Spanish magic, it has nothing to do with religion. Believing in God is about heaven and hell, right and wrong. Spanish magic is neutral," he told me. "It is only about solving problems in your life and protecting yourself from your enemies. You have to make sure and curse them before they curse you, or find a prayer strong enough to make their stuff bounce back to them. It has nothing to do with religion." Divination and witchcraft were not a part of their religion, in my friends' minds, which is why their mother could be seen as very religious in two spheres: her dedication to attending mass, and her intimate knowledge of the spirit world. You can begin to see the way in which their experience with Christianity, by failing to account for the myths of spiritual power, completely overlooked major facets of the life of this family.

For many North Americans, the myth of spiritual power feels the most foreign. We might not even recognize the degree to which it is swirling all around us on a regular basis. We may be serving cross-culturally among a diaspora community where the myth of spiritual power is prevalent, but we may fail to recognize its influence and the significance of the symbols, language, or stories that we encounter because we lack experience in this cultural world. Historically, in our modern Western context, scientific inquiry took place in the public domain while religion became a private and individualized matter. Natural laws took precedence for explaining every day matters while God's territory was limited to heaven, hell, and eternal matters. As a consequence, there was little space for supernatural activities or mystic powers to be at work in our present world. However, in many cultures and subcultures these practices never actually went way. Rather they continue though perhaps as a hidden layer of religious practice, on the margins of religious institutions, or as a syncretistic blend (Hiebert et al., 2000, pp. 16–20).

Despite the lack of attention typically given, at least publically, to this myth within Western cultures, the Scriptures are not shy about wading into the world of spiritual powers. Jesus is not shy about confronting spiritual powers, and Paul identifies, in Ephesians 6, that our struggle is "not against flesh and blood." He naturally declares Jesus as the Lord of all things in creation—both visible and invisible (Colossians 1:16). For many Christians in the United States, much of the language and perception by the writers of the Bible is culturally foreign to our contemporary perception of the world around us. While we should remain sensitive to our own cultural assumptions, our Bibles continue to provide our best resource for addressing the myth of spiritual powers.

As we reach out to our diaspora neighbors, it is important that we learn to listen for the myth of spiritual powers. Indeed, many missionaries have committed to the worthwhile study of world religions that they would inevitably encounter, only to find that many of the everyday people they meet have little real understanding of the formal religion they claim for themselves (Hiebert et al., 2000, p. 19). However, the myth of spiritual powers typically persists in its various cultural forms even where religious orthodoxy falls short.

Practice One

Case Study

In one of your evangelistic small groups, the facilitator is a new Christian named Simon. During his faith journey, Simon spent a lot of time studying the Gnostic gospels and the philosophy of Daoism. One day while reading a biblical passage referring to angels, Simon began to share about a time he believed he made contact with extraterrestrials. Another new Christian in the group, Johnny, corrects him, saying that there is no other life in the universe apart from God, humans, angels, and demons. Simon does not believe that spiritual beings would make contact in this way; you assume this may tie into his high regard for Gnostic theology. This ignites a lively debate in the whole group about their various experiences making contact with non-human life: some consider these spiritual beings and some alien life. You quickly realize that every member of this church has some first-hand experience of such things, and these beliefs hold deep emotional significance to each of them. Finding that they have irreconcilable differences in their experiences, they turn to you to settle the matter.

Reflect on how you might answer their question about whether Christians can believe in and experience other beings. Identify in what ways these experiences may have caused them to hear or interpret Scripture differently from yourself. How would Scripture address these themes? Select a few passages that address this area that might be helpful to study together in the next few church meetings.

Notes:

Practice Two

Case Study

In one of your house-churches, you are studying the story of the prodigal son (Luke 15:11:32). One of the newest attendees is a former Muslim from Montenegro who is now highly secular and has a high opinion of his scientific training. Another member, Michel, is Latino and his role as a leader and pastoral figure is very much entangled in the inclusive character of this church. When discussing the passage, your Montenegrin friend makes a comment about forgiveness similar to a discussion you had in this group the week before, when he was not in attendance. Upon hearing this, Michael grows excited and decides to point out the similarity of your perspective to your new friend. "Bro," he says, "you don't even know this yet, but the Holy Spirit put those words in your mind and you didn't even know what you were saying. If you keep coming, you'll learn the way it works, but that's so awesome that the spirit is already speaking through you and you don't even realize it." You can tell that, on various levels, this has not been well received by the new member.

Identify the way in which the myth of spiritual powers is involved and how you might respond without violating the myth of inclusion that is so central to this group's character as a community. Reflect on how you might engage the different spiritual myths in the moment and in follow up with both members in question.

Notes:

Practice Three

Case Study

While exploring a South Asian neighborhood in another part of your city, you walk into a Pakistani restaurant for lunch. Looking up at the wall you see that it is covered with beautiful Arabic calligraphy, most likely a passage from the Qur'an. You tell the owner of the shop how much you like his decoration and, in an attempt to start up a spiritual conversation, you ask him what it means. "Oh," he says, "that is a verse from the Qur'an. But I cannot read it. I know what the sounds of the words are but I do not know the meaning." It is not uncommon for Muslims to learn Arabic phonetically but have no working vocabulary, so this fact does not surprise you. Seeking not to lose the thread of the conversation, though, you ask him why he chose this verse if he cannot read it. He replies, "Everyone knows that it is good luck to have such a thing in a new business. It keeps the bad spirits away and brings you success." Identify the way in which the myth of powers is operating here and how this might affect your Gospel presentation with this shop owner.

Notes:

Practice Four

Case Study

One of your emerging church leaders is a former employee of a crystal shop and an herbalist. When he first became a Christian he was a highly involved in various New Age practices, using these elements when engaging the spiritual world. Several months ago, however, he came to you and said, "Even though I still I recommend herbs to people for their health, I understand that those things have no power other than what God has put in nature. God is the only one who heals and who is worthy of worship, but that means that created things are still helpful when placed under His lordship." This seems to be a reasonably healthy perspective at this point in his journey as a new disciple.

Recently your friend has begun discipling a group of neighbors in his home across town. While you are thrilled that he is so evangelistically inclined, you also recognize that many of his neighbors are Caribbean Latinos and have a familiarity if not a personal history with Santeria and other spiritual practices of the occult. The use of many of the same plants your friend recommends are tied into the rituals of Santeria and are used for summoning certain spirits. While secular friends would view these herbs from a purely biological perspective, his neighbors may associate them with spiritual practices. How do you help him navigate his new-found "freedom from idols" when it may be a stumbling block to new believers who adhere to myths of spiritual power?

Notes:

Chapter 12

Holidays, Culture on Display

I (Seth) remember celebrating Columbus Day as a school holiday. We did not know much about Columbus, but we saw this as a chance to celebrate the origins of our country. We associated with the holiday stories of the explorers' tenacity and innovation.as positive models for the values of our nation. My sister is more than a decade younger than me. By the time she was in school, Columbus Day was no longer a priority in the school calendar. By this point, Martin Luther King Junior's birthday had become a holiday, with Dr. King exemplifying values that made our culture great: a love of liberty, a belief in the equality of all people, and a defense of truth and justice against opposition. When I moved to New York, once again I saw Columbus Day celebrated enthusiastically, as the Italian diaspora held a big parade running the length of Central Park with many people wearing traditional costumes and waving the Italian flag. In this context, Columbus was celebrated as a symbol of Italian culture.

Several years ago when I (Jared) first started planting a church in New York City, I was well aware of the importance of holidays. At the time there was a general consensus in the church planting world that Easter Sunday was the ideal time to launch a new assembly. While there are plenty of New Yorkers who return to church on Easter

Sunday, the people we were trying to reach seemed more inclined to celebrate at home with extended family than to attend a religious service. Some of those we were reaching could go back two or three generations of their family and still find no meaningful participation in a church community. Those who did attend were more likely to make an annual pilgrimage to their mother's or grandmother's church — often the last church they had visited—than to attend the start of a new church meeting in a public school facility. We discovered that the first Sunday after New Year's Day was a much more likely time for the people we were reaching to consider visiting a new church. Although the

middle of winter in the Northeast U.S. seems an unlikely time to start a church, New Year's Day is the time when people are engaged in self-reflection and making resolutions—including getting themselves right with God. In an urban, multiethnic, individualistic crowd, we discovered that New Year's functions as a spiritual holiday that was often full of meaning as an opportunity for new beginnings.

In other cultural settings even in the same city, Easter would maintain important religious significance. Passover, Eid, and other religious events are often filled with spiritual meaning or nostalgia for the participants. A key task for cross-cultural workers is to discover the days and events that possess meaning and include important rituals for their cultural group. They must pay attention to the ways that ministry activities or evangelistic dialog may intersect with these moments, and as learners, they should recognize how holidays offer rich learning opportunities for studying the culture.

Holidays are the pageantry of culture. The values and myths of culture are translated into spectacle in order to commemorate, legitimize, and reinforce those myths and to communicate to the spectator the allegiances and identity of the celebrators (Foucault, 1997). Rituals and religious festivals sustain faith and express culture in a way doctrinal explanations simply cannot. If cross-cultural evangelists desire to see the Gospel plant deep roots among a people, they need to take seriously the significance of religious celebrations and rituals (Hiebert et al., 2000, p. 283).

If we are careful observers in the participation of our diaspora neighbors' holidays, there is much we can learn about the culture's myths that may be less visible or less comprehensible at other times. For example, the Hindu celebration of Durga Puja includes a reenactment of the god Durga's defeat of the great buffalo demon Mahishasura and, according to our Hindu friends, epitomizes the struggle of good overcoming evil. In the dramatic reenactment, Durga is formed and equipped by the gods with a weapon in each of her many hands to slay the demon. At the end of the play when Durga finally kills Mahishasura, we can rejoice because we anticipate the way that good will overcome evil in the world (Chamberlain, 2002, p. 30).

In observing this holiday, we see not only myths about the spirit world but also the myth of redemptive violence (Wink, 1992)— that it is divine conquest that ushers in peace—that the gods use warfare as a means of subduing or controlling the chaos which breaks out in our world. How might these myths affect this culture's approach to conflict and chaos? How might understanding these myths help us contrast the message of the Gospel in our retelling? How does knowledge of the celebration's timing with the harvest affect our interpretation of its origins and meaning? Does the celebration of Durga Puja as a dramatic reenactment teach us any lessons about what good formal contextualization might look like as Hindu background people experience conversion to Christian faith?

A less dramatic example might be the birthday celebration we attended for our friend Adya. When we arrived an hour late for the party, we assumed that we were being wise in regards to our understanding of the myths concerning relational versus event-oriented attitudes toward time in Bengali culture (Lingenfelter, 2003, pp. 37–42). However, as we entered her apartment a group of older women were finishing their meal and preparing to leave. We feared we had misjudged and arrived too late: maybe this was a party just for women or maybe we were actually supposed to show up at 6:00 pm. Adya welcomed us in, however, and we were immediately instructed to begin eating. After half an hour the next guests arrived. These were her friends and coworkers who she spent much of her free time with. They stayed for a few hours and begin to depart in small clusters while the next group began to trickle in. The third wave of the party consisted of Adya's boss and his business partner and their families. The guests with the highest status had waited until the party was well underway before arriving. They sat, ate and, after some polite conversation and the cutting of the cake, got their children ready to depart. At this point it was almost 1:00 in the morning. The last guests to arrive were those friends who did not get off of work until late in the evening. When we left at 2:00 in the morning, the party showed no sign of winding down.

What myths about social status can we see through this experience? What are the myths about time? How do you determine where you fit into the social spectrum and what expectations there might be of you in conjunction with this identity? How similar is this experience to depictions of parties we see in the New Testament? How do these similarities or differences open opportunities to share the Gospel?

Practice One

Cultural Study

List the major holidays and celebrations of your neighbor's culture:

1.

2.

3.

4.

5.

In what ways do these celebrations provide a sense of continuity with this culture's past? This is one of the major functions of holidays, to reinforce identification with the past through tradition and repetition (e.g., Thanksgiving, Fourth of July). Identify the contextual origins behind each of these celebrations. Some common appeals in our experience are:

- Appeals to agriculture or husbandry (e.g., Sukkot, Thanksgiving)
- Appeals to historical figures and events (e.g., Bastille Day, July 4th, Martin Luther King Day)
- Appeals to religious myths (e.g., Passover, Eid)

Discuss how you might utilize these concepts in discussing Christian holidays? How might the celebrations of your diaspora neighbor's culture provide openings to share about the different holidays we see in Scripture?

Notes:

Chapter 13

Myths About Time

Time is a complex and multifaceted subject. Specialists in various fields of cultural studies have written much about time and reflected upon diverse case studies from around the world. Our focus in this section is to help cross-cultural evangelists working in multicultural cities gain some practical handles on time as they engage a diverse sea of cultures living and working in their metropolitan region. In our experience and observations, we have identified two primary mythic areas concerning time:

Myths about "Real" Time

Time is Scarce: Event Orientation

It is important that I don't waste my time. I grow impatient when I show up to a social event or to church and it is delayed. When a speaker goes over her allotted time, it is easy to feel that the audience becomes anxious. Efficiency is a key way to respect people's time and lateness is a sign of not respecting how busy everyone else is. When I schedule meetings, if something comes up which will delay me for more than 20 minutes it is most polite to reschedule rather than make my associate wait.

Time is Abundant: Relational Orientation

Life is unpredictable and many delays may occur outside my control. If someone tells me they will meet me at a certain time, I help them save face by expecting this may not be the case. Who knows what will happen that day to delay them? This is why it is important to value relationships above the events that bring us together. If a public speaker is especially good, she should keep going. A party should be well underway before the guests of honor arrive, and if they are delayed, we will wait for them. The longer we wait, the more honored they will feel when they arrive. In doing this, we do not shame those who may be delayed for reasons beyond their control and we honor those who understand that we value them above our schedules.

Myths about Historical time

Time is Ending: Eschatological Orientation

During the course of history God's purposes have been accomplished and are coming to fulfillment. For this reason, the defining aspect of our lives is where we will spend eternity. Our focus in this life should extend beyond our time on earth and we should not be preoccupied by present things, as they are inconsequential in light of the eternal. Given the fact that we do not know when God will come in judgment, we should not focus so much on our present lives, as if the end will occur in the distant future. The end could come at any time. Time is not guaranteed and should be prioritized with the end of all things in mind.

Time is Advancing: Progressive Orientation

History is advancing towards an increasingly better future for humanity. In the past, humanity was less knowledgeable about our world and the things we know now had yet to be discovered or revealed. Technology, medicine, natural sciences, human psychology, sexuality, and so many areas of our contemporary world were poorly understood in the past, and the future holds similar changes we can only imagine. Our orientation, then, is towards seeking to be on the right side of history. We do this through making decisions in keeping with the progress we expect to see in the future. To lose sight of our place in the progression of history is to lose touch with moral authority.

Time is Recurring: Cyclical Orientation

Life holds the same struggle for each generation; the best that we can ask of ourselves is that we learn from the wisdom of those who came before us and that we recognize the cosmic patterns that are destined to recur. The way to make peace with the passing of time is to recognize our place in the cycle and accept the role we must play in our context. History is something we can expect to see recur in our own lives. We should seek to act as faithfully as we can in light of the fruit we have seen borne by the previous generations in similar circumstances.

Thinking about "Real" Time

When I (Jared) was growing up, my family was sometimes late for church. By late, I mean ten minutes late. Even so, we generally arrived prior to the opening song and seldom was anyone among our church membership more than ten minutes late. Our worship services typically finished on-the-minute, just as they began.

In my twenties, I served as a junior member of a ministry team planting a church cross-culturally in an impoverished urban community in the Southern U.S. In contrast with my childhood experience, we would sing and pray for an extended period while members of the church would trickle in over the course of an hour or more. We would begin the assembly with two dozen people, which swelled to over a hundred by the time the sermon and testimonies began, well into the service. Some readers will relate to the first story while others will resonate with the second one. Each example reflects a different cultural experience with time.

When I was a child, we spent many Thanksgiving celebrations and Christmas dinners at my grandparent's home. If dinner was planned for 1:00, we generally arrived on time, but certainly no later than 1:30. It was never articulated as a hard and fast rule and we didn't put much thought into it—that's just how we did things. Later, as a young new missionary in New York City, I bonded with local believers who acted as my cultural informants while I adapted to life in the outer boroughs of an incredibly international city. A culturally mixed couple from Puerto Rico and Trinidad invited me to Thanksgiving at their home, and I joyfully accepted. Dinner was scheduled for three o'clock in the afternoon, so I jumped on the subway and showed up at the front door of their home promptly at three. After helping run an errand to the grocery store, I sat and watched the four o'clock football game until around seven p.m. when the rest of the family began to arrive. Dinner eventually began as we shared a blend of West Indian foods and the typical American dishes of the season. It was an enjoyable evening that afforded me several opportunities to share my hope in Christ with their extended family. By eleven o'clock, I had been in their home for eight hours and was more than ready to go home; however, at this point, they turned on the radio and started a card game. The night was still young! My gracious hosts and I were operating with different time orientations. Up to that point, I had failed to make necessary adjustments. Most missionaries reading this can easily relate to this experience and laugh at my cultural miscues.

I (Jared) have to confess that adapting to different perspectives regarding time has been one of the most difficult adjustments for me as an urban missionary in a multicultural city. In cross-cultural ministry, we bear the responsibility to move beyond our ethnocentric tendencies and to humble ourselves to the standards and expectations of the host culture. I eventually adapted, but it has required more, well, *time* than I would hope to admit. Truthfully, cross-cultural ministry raises challenges that are both strategic and personal. Even as we enjoy immersing ourselves in the cultural diversity of our city, taking seriously the demands of incarnational ministry sometimes stretches us where we least expect it.

Time Zones

We like to think of the differing perspectives about time we encounter in the city as working in different "time zones." For the cross-cultural worker in a multicultural city, one question to ask is: 'What time zone am I in?' In a multicultural city there will likely be a variety of orientations to time operating simultaneously within the same urban space. Even within the same community, there may be different time zones at work. Members of a diaspora community may implicitly understand that they are living in multiple time zones— whether or not they would articulate it as such. The city is an engine in the global economy where markets are tightly linked to schedules and calendars to the day, minute, and second. However, cultural events are likely to run on a different schedule given the specific orientations of particular cultures or subcultures.

Many of our diaspora neighbors know that they must treat professional time with precision if they are to advance or at least maintain their career within the modern economy. Therefore, they adjust to that time zone and understand when they are working in that space. Yet, cultural festivities usually do not place the same restraints upon participants, and depending on the culture involved, it is not uncommon for attendees to come and go over many hours. It is not unusual for my wife and me (Jared) intentionally to head to a party in our neighborhood an hour or more after the official start time in order to be "on time"—and still find ourselves among the first to arrive. However, our hosts would have a different set of expectations if we were collaborating together in institutional activities such as business or education. For instance, we have been involved with friends in educational projects in the community where everyone was expected to arrive at a specific time and move through academic sessions within a rigid timeframe. We have attended neighborhood parties with the same friends where it is customary to arrive two or three hours after the announced start time of the event and allow people to trickle in throughout the day or evening. Those are distinct time zones operating within the city. Time may be based on the country of origin, on professional expectations, or a hybrid blending the varied experiences of a diaspora people. Cross-cultural ministers reaching out to diaspora communities in global cities are tasked with deciphering the time zone in which they are currently operating.

Missionaries working in rural areas of Africa, Latin America, or other corners of the world where a single culture is represented, there is likely a single time expectation at work in that culture, especially in traditional settings. However, in a globalized, multicultural city, missionaries may need to adjust to differing time expectations depending on the impact of a dominant culture and related professional settings, the characteristics of a cultural hybrid, or alternative time expectations of a diaspora subculture. They must navigate diverse and varied cultural settings and expectations. For cross-cultural evangelists in the city, negotiating time is not as static as one would expect to find in a more monocultural or traditional society. Instead of a single expectation of time, approaches to time may vary from diaspora to diaspora and result in hybrids negotiating between expectations of the marketplace and expectations of a particular ethnic culture.

After a refugee friend from Liberia had lived in New York City for some months, he declared, "Jared, everything in America is bound by time. In my country, we had more flexibility, but here you must always be on time. There is so much pressure because of time." Michael Laguerre says the treatment of time is a key aspect of assimilation and resistance to Western settings for international migrants. He explains that each diaspora community is struggling for "the preservation of its cultural heritage while at the same time being shaped by and contributing to the mainstream." The global city becomes a place of multiple calendars each claiming its own cultural rhythms but unavoidably being affected by the scheduling practices of the dominant culture and demands of a global economy. One must pay attention to the immigrant's time because it informs the rhythm of socialization in the new country, the speed with which adaptation occurs, group conflicts between different perceptions of time, generational conflicts among parents and children, diasporic holy days and holidays, and the recognition of different temporal perspectives within a given nation. Migrants from the majority world often need to adjust their life rhythms in regards to time in their new American cities. Yet, this adjustment does not remain static. Life within the diaspora network and interactions with kinship networks back home prompt them to negotiate between differing time zones. As migrants in the city learn to navigate the temporal demands of their host city and the natural rhythms of their culture of origin, they develop a cultural hybrid approach for the sake of their own well-being, enabling them to interact across differing expectations of time (Laguerre, 2003, pp. 6–27).

American culture tends to see time as finite and as a utility; we even attach moral value to one's "use" of time. Take, for example, the rules governing punctuality. Arriving 1 to 3 minutes after the allotted time without explanation is acceptable; 5-10 minutes late is also acceptable but usually requires an apology; 15-25 minutes late requires some justification for one's lateness; anything beyond this is considered rude enough that it would be better to reschedule or not meet at all. By contrast, consider the perception of time in much of the majority world, which we can see exemplified by my friend Salam. When we hang out, I (Seth) have always waited at least 30 minutes beyond the agreed time for Salam to arrive. It is not unusual for me to sit alone in a coffee shop or restaurant for an hour before he texts to say whether he still plans to honor our agreement to meet or not.

While cities in North America function as secular space, we can often observe significant diversity in management of time and treatment of special religious days. Many cultures living in the same metropolitan area results in multiple calendars. For example, in New York Muslims mark Fridays and other special days for prayer; Jews close shops early on Friday afternoon for Sabbath; Protestant Christians observe Sunday as a sacred day, while Catholic mass is performed throughout the week, with special emphasis on Sunday mass. Despite this diversity, the civil day of rest remains Sunday, demonstrating the historical influence of the Christian calendar in the American context (Laguerre, 2003, pp. 28–36). Stepping into cross-cultural ministry among diaspora communities, we encounter a world of diversity and constant change. In order to navigate between the expectations associated with different contexts and circumstances, it is essential to discern which time zone is operating.

Thinking about Historical Time

Time is Ending

Not long ago, we were teaching a class on ethnographic research to a group of new missionaries who had come to be part of a cross-cultural training program in New York City. The city is an amazing classroom for experiencing any number of new cultures. At the start of the class we asked the participants to share any new experiences they had had while adjusting to life in a large global city like New York.

One of the participants described sharing her faith in Christ with a fellow passenger on the subway. She attempted to present the importance of choosing between heaven or hell for our eternal destination, an issue certainly discussed in Scripture as a critical concern. However, her fellow passenger, a member of the vast Chinese diaspora in New York, responded by letting her know that she had never contemplated heaven, hell, or even eternity in general. These simply were not things that she thought about; her concerns were generally for the present. This new missions student said with astonishment, "I've never talked with anyone who thinks that way." For the student, myths about time coming to a completion were primary, so it was difficult even to imagine how to share the good news with someone who didn't value the same myths. Of course, we know the Gospel speaks frequently to our concerns of eternal life; however, it also certainly has plenty to say about Kingdom life in our world right now. Our starting point for sharing the good news with another culture must be a contextual bridge that makes sense not only to us, but more importantly, to our hearer. Given her Chinese neighbor's presently-oriented view of historical time, the Gospel's implications for the "here and now" may have been a better initial myth from which to build a bridge as a starting point, reserving the important discussion about the resurrection and eternal hope for a later point in their dialog. In temporal myths, as in so many areas, the question is not whether the individual with whom we're sharing the Gospel has "the right myths," it is more of a question of how to begin with the most effective bridges for communicating good news.

When communicating the message of the Gospel with our international neighbors, we don't want our own natural default positions to become a barrier to our diaspora neighbors. Time is one area where the balance of contextualization may be most difficult, perhaps because it is one of the mythic areas most taken for granted by a culture. It had never occurred to this missionary student that, for her conversation partner, historical time did not have an end point at which God would determine people's eternal life. It had never occurred to her Chinese neighbor that time was moving towards any eternal result. These differences are best explained as a difference of myths about time, but that divergence is critical for the presentation of the Gospel. As Vincent Donovan says, "The Gospel is, after all, not a philosophy or set of doctrines or laws. That is what a culture is. The Gospel is essentially a history, at whose center is the God-man born in Bethlehem, risen near Golgotha" (Donovan, 1978, p. 24). Therefore, we want to be attentive both to others' and to our own theological orientations of time without sacrificing our testimony to the truth of what God has done in history as well as the hope He offers.

Time Is Progressing

Many Americans possess myths of historical time we might characterize as linear. A linear view of time views history—both personal and global—as a progression of events moving towards an end. However, rather than an extra-temporal and spiritual end, the end of a linear time line is achieved through a process of historical improvement. This generally results in the construction of narratives about societal and moral progress when reviewing history and causes us to ascribe meaning to the chronology of particular events.

Myths of linear time often lead us to be optimistic about the future and the ability of society to improve over time. We tend to view past societies as less sophisticated and thus, less authoritative than our own (Manchester & Reid, 2012, pp. 20–21). We also seek to view ourselves from the perspective of those who will follow after us historically; how our grandchildren will judge us is of more central concern than what our ancestors would say. We desire to be "on the right side of history," so we make decisions by orienting ourselves towards the future. In essence, our temporal myths push us to value historical progress and to be "progressive" in our judgments.

Time is Recurring

In contrast to a progression of time, we find that some of our majority world friends, such as those who are Hindu, understand time to be cyclical. They tend to focus on the present time in relation to patterns or cycles derived from the past. Although they plan for their families' immediate futures, they do not strongly identify with or value the future. In this view, the past tends to be depersonalized. In conversation with Hindus in New York City, we have been unable to establish the historical origins of their holidays and customs despite their strong narrative orientation. This approach to time contrasts significantly with our American Christian narratives that are connected to historical events, people, and places. Similarly our American national holidays are almost all attached to easily identifiable historical events or persons. A culture with a cyclical view of time does not need to rely on its understanding of history or vision of the future to provide a foundation for identity.

Each view of time presents its own challenges for cross-cultural evangelists. As we reach out to diverse communities in our cities, we must note what time zone is operating in a specific situation or context. This may help us adjust our ministry expectations realistically and determine the most effective bridges to Gospel-centered conversations.

Practice One

Scripture Study

In the following Scripture, identify myths about time and the ways this text might present a bridge or a barrier in interacting with the various conceptions of time discussed above:

> There is a season for everything and a time for every matter under the heavens: a time for giving birth and a time for dying, a time for planting and a time for uprooting what was planted, a time for killing and a time for healing, a time for tearing down and a time for building up, a time for crying and a time for laughing, a time for mourning and a time for dancing, a time for throwing stones and a time for gathering stones, a time for embracing and a time for avoiding embraces, a time for searching and a time for losing, a time for keeping and a time for throwing away, a time for tearing and a time for repairing, a time for keeping silent and a time for speaking, a time for loving and a time for hating, a time for war and a time for peace. What do workers gain from all their hard work? I have observed the task that God has given human beings. God has made everything fitting in its time, but has also placed eternity in their hearts, without enabling them to discover what God has done from beginning to end. I know that there is nothing better for them but to enjoy themselves and do what is good while they live. Moreover, this is the gift of God: that all people should eat, drink, and enjoy the results of their hard work. I know that whatever God does will last forever; it is impossible to add to it or take away from it. God has done this so that people are reverent before him. Whatever happens has already

happened, and whatever will happen has already happened before. And God looks after what is driven away (Ecc. 3:1–15 CEB).

Notes:

Practice Two

Time in the Gospels

In thinking about Jesus's ministry, discuss the ways in which his social interactions demonstrated or challenged the following:

Event Oriented Time:

Relationally Oriented Time:

Discuss the way that the Messianic expectation in the community of Jesus's time may have corresponded to or challenged the following:

Myths about the end of time:

Myths about the progression of time:

Myths about recurrence of time:

Practice Three

Case Study

You have volunteered to help tutor a young Arab man in conversational English. He has always arrived on time and your sessions are efficient and end promptly. As your relationship has developed, however, you have begun to schedule times to meet for coffee outside of regular tutoring. Your friend has yet to arrive at any of these meetings within any reasonable timeframe. He is chronically 30-50 minutes late, which turns a simple coffee into an all-afternoon event for you. How do you interpret this difference in behavior based on what you have learned in the previous chapter? What, if anything, will you do to engage your friend about this scheduling difficulty?

Follow up: Your friend has invited you to a meal at his home. How do you know what time zone to operate in for this occasion? What are the risks you take in misjudging the time zone?

Practice Four

Case Study

You have a Bible study with a group of young professionals who are natives of the city. Within the group there are mixed feelings about religion, but there appear to be three camps in the group's orientation towards the future: the first believes that through following Jesus as a moral teacher we can steadily improve ourselves until we arrive at a near idyllic community; the second believes that Jesus's teachings are helpful, but that because of its historical context much of the Bible's moral teachings are less developed than our own and we can disregard them—particularly as it applies to the understanding of sexuality in Scripture; the third party takes a strong interest in geopolitics and believes that we can use current events to discern how close we are to the end of days.

Identify the narratives involved in each party's view. Discuss whether or not the myths of progress in these views is an appropriate framework through which to understand the Gospel or an obstacle that must be challenged.

Notes:

Chapter 14

Christ Among the Myths

Up to this point we have wanted to allow the reader space to observe and reflect on the suggested myths for themselves. An important part of our discipleship methodology is to leave space for the learner to reflect and come to decisions with minimal interference from the facilitator's opinions. We have thus tried to pay the same respect to you as our reader. At this time, however, we would like to reflect on some of the ways we see Christ interacting with the myths being discussed. These myths are expressed in a variety of ways in culture, and this leads to a variety of resolutions. However, some mythic values and roles can be identified that transcend cultures when we speak about the intersection of Gospel and culture. We would like to evaluate some of these points of proximity here.

In the figure below, we outline how we see these myths interacting with the Gospel. It is important to emphasize that every culture may be both affirmed and challenged by the Gospel in different ways that are specific to that culture. As we encounter these myths playing out in different manners in each subculture as we serve our communities in increasingly diverse cities, the Gospel confronts each of these myths. As a cross-cultural evangelist, we have the task of discovering how the message of Christ challenges and brings hope. The

Mosaic

Scriptures suggested in this chart are not meant as exhaustive but as a starting point for allowing the Bible to speak to various cultural myths. Going forward in this chapter, we hope to highlight some ways we might respond to each of these cultural myths as we engage different peoples within our cities.

Figure 7: Christ Among the Myths						
Myth	Primary Value	Mythic Desire	Primary Fear	Gospel Hope	Role of Christ	Scripture to Share
Empire	Idealization of One's Own Culture	Restoration/ Actualization of Ideal	Loss of Cultural Values Within Structures of Power	Universal Kingdom	Self-Emptying King	John 18
Inclusion	Solidarity with Group	Obtain Honor for the Group	The Group Acquiring Shame	Adoption into God's Favor	Proper Measure of Acceptance/Identity	Philippians 2
Law	Establishing Correct Social Framework	To Live Appropriately	Violating the Framework Right Living	Freedom From/For	Definitive Interpreter and Model	Matthew 5
Spiritual Power	Harmony with Spiritual World	Security in Face of Spiritual Powers	Loss of Security/Harmony	Ransom from Powers	Authority over all Powers	Colossians 2
Linear Time	Progress of History	Be on the Right Side of History	Losing Moral Perspective	Birth of a New Age	Climax of History	1 Corinthians 2
Cyclical Time	Harmony with Cosmic Cycle	To Find One's Place	To Be Out of Balance/To Obset Divine Order	Birth of a New Age	Template and Telos of Creation	Romans 8

The Myth of Empire

The basic values and desires of imperial myths are centered around the belief that one's own culture is founded upon a set of ideals which represent the pinnacle of human well-being. At times the myth is used by the oppressed who long for liberation and restoration; at other times the myth is used to sustain existing systems of power and identify a scapegoated party that is accused of undermining the values that make the culture great. Either way, the intention of the myth of empire is the preservation and idealization of cultural values as expressed in social systems of power. The desire, then, for both the powerful and the downtrodden is the actualization of these same ideals within the political sphere.

How does the Gospel intersect with the myth of Empire? We would suggest that the primary way it engages this myth is in the universality of God's Kingdom. In his ongoing mission God is calling people of every culture and tribe and nation to participate in a new kind of Kingdom—a Kingdom that both subverts the old ideals but also preserves those elements that are reflections of God's own nature. There are aspects of every culture that are challenged by the good news of God's Kingdom, and there are aspects of every culture that are affirmed by his Kingdom. The Kingdom we see at the realization of God's mission, then, is both not of this world but is also representative of the best of this world.

Jesus enters incarnationally into the myth of empire, adopting its language and categories to help explain his mission. Ultimately, however, Jesus uses this mythic incarnation to subvert the imperial myth itself. In the myth of empire Jesus is not only the king of the new Kingdom, but he is the king who refuses to be defined by any ideals but those of the Father. Jesus is a king who refuses to seek after or use power as a force of coercion, a king who loves and forgives his enemies and has no need to utilize violence to protect the values or identity of his people. He is the king of a Kingdom greater than any other principality, kingdom, or empire. God's Kingdom exists in the same space as the nations but subverts them all for the sake of God's redemptive mission (Wink, 1992).

The Myth of Inclusion

Inclusive myths pertain to one's status within the community and the community's status in the eyes of its neighbors. In it, desires and fears center on notions of honor and shame as primary metrics of value. The Gospel addresses inclusive myths by identifying Jesus as the proper judge of honor and shame. The ultimate honor, adoption by God, is accomplished by allegiance to Jesus and the ultimate shame, divine rejection, is the result of rejecting Jesus. One's own cultural identity is affirmed within God's good creation while at the same time finding our ultimate identity in the global family of God.

A Gospel presentation of Jesus engaging the myth of inclusion points out that when God spoke as the prophet Jesus, there were many religious leaders who felt that what Jesus said and did brought shame on the community. Feeling a duty to preserve the honor of God's people, they asked Jesus many trick questions to trap him in situations that would shame him in the eyes of the people. When they could not shame or discredit Jesus, they decided to kill him as a blasphemer to remove the shame he had brought to them and the dishonor they believed he had brought to God. However, by raising Jesus from the dead, God demonstrated that the religious leaders has shamed themselves by ignoring the teaching of Jesus, and we bring shame on ourselves when we believe that Jesus does not speak for God. Rather than focusing solely upon the cross as a symbol of sacrifice, we may also see the cross as God's willingness to absorb our shame and to vindicate Jesus through the resurrection. Even if it brings us honor in our neighbors' eyes we actually dishonor our whole community before God when we say that he has not spoken through Jesus.

Understanding communities with highly inclusive myths might cause us to give greater attention to the propensity for disciples to reject and be rejected by family. It also might cause us to highlight the need for disciples to not do their acts of righteousness to be seen by others, but to seek to take the lowest place. Due to our highly individualistic culture, the inclusive myth may be the most overlooked by Western missionaries, but it is also presents the easiest contextualization possibilities, as it is very much a primary myth in the cultural world of the New Testament.

Myths of the Law

Legalistic myths are deeply concerned with living in harmony with the correct social framework. They are frequently seen as the primary means of preserving the stability of a society. For Americans this is often a matter of egalitarian social legislation—ensuring that every individual is treated equally. For East and South Asians, it is often a matter of living correctly within social hierarchy and caste. Europeans tend to blend classist and democratic frameworks in their legal myths, depending on whether national or social relationships are the matter in question. For our Chinese and Korean friends, respect for authority and proper titles are central values linked to the legal myth.

For Muslims, social hierarchy as well as proper observance of religious law are integral to the legal myth. For many Western Christians, proper education and ordination are central to the myth of law. Each culture expresses this myth in various narratives and structures (Kraft, 2008, pp. 386–390).

The Gospel addresses this legalistic desire for appropriate living by setting up Jesus as the definitive interpreter of both religious law as well as the proper model for the use of authority. The fact that Jesus refuses to lord his authority over others and teaches his disciples to do the same challenges the legal myths that would uphold hierarchy as a necessary part of following Jesus. The way in which Jesus both affirms and dramatically deepens the intention of *Torah* in his Sermon on the Mount gives good news and guidance to those for whom legal myths are a means of seeking the proper way to live in relationship to God. Myths of law are one of the areas that are most difficult for Americans to relinquish in order to acknowledge a legitimate diversity of perspective with regard to our international neighbor. Legal myths, however, are also the area where our culture is probably furthest from the perspective of the Gospel writers.

Myths of Spiritual Power

In recent years, myths of spiritual power have gone through a resurgence in the American church, with the rise of Pentecostalism and greater exposure to stories of dramatic spiritual encounters in the churches of the Majority World. Whether we refer to the folk–Islamic practice of North Africans, the everyday encounters of American charismatic Christians, or the magical rites of Santeria among Latino diasporas, people who follow spiritualist myths desire to live in harmony with entities operating in the spiritual realm. Myths of spiritual power see the problems of the everyday - money, health, relationship - as having their solutions in the spiritual world (De La Torre, 2004, p. 5). This desire for harmony often produces fear as the need for security becomes the primary purpose of spiritual practice. Fear and power, then, become the poles that define the worlds of those motivated by myths of spiritual power.

The Gospel addresses this issue in the figure of Jesus who has authority over both the physical and spiritual world. Jesus, as the Christ, can not only drive out demons and heal the sick, but, through his death and resurrection, has unmasked the principalities and powers in a way which takes away the need to fear their authority (Wink, 1992). Allegiance to Jesus, then, places us under the authority of one who has power beyond that of all other authorities, relieving the need to seek after other forms of security in relation to the spiritual world. Another facet of this myth's Gospel presentation is God's sending the church the Holy Spirit as a comforter and guide. Christians have no need to consult other spiritual powers or seek out other sources of spiritual wisdom because God has supplied what is needed for those who follow Jesus.

Myths of Linear Time

In myths that value historical progress, people tend to orient themselves towards the future. Historical advancement is the standard of judgment, and societies of the past are seen as possessing less sophisticated moral and intellectual frameworks. From the perspective of this myth, we have evolved beyond the ability for Scripture to reveal to us what is true, or real, or good. We have created other structures

227

that are capable of answering those questions for us–in light of these, Jesus often seems superfluous and church appears atavistic. This is at odds with the picture we see in the Gospel of Jesus as the climax of God's action in history. In Jesus, God has begun a new age which will subsume and overtake the flow of history and never be surpassed in its revelation of the divine.

Presenting the Gospel in this myth may require demonstrating the ways in which, despite our advances in technology and anthropological perspective, human beings still operate out of the same brokenness Jesus addresses in his own time. Despite our societal accomplishments, human nature remains constant. Our societies have not advanced beyond the very seeds of destruction Jesus prophetically calls to account in his own world, nor have we created means of evolving beyond the sort of community he seeks to initiate among his disciples. Despite the areas of progress society appears to be making, we have not advanced to the world Jesus challenges us to envision as it exists in the Kingdom of God.

Myths of Cyclical Time

The desire of cyclical myths of time is to be in harmony with and to find one's place in the cycle of history. For many people this results in a fear of upsetting the balance or order of life and anything beyond the immediate future is given little thought. Presenting the Gospel in this myth, then, requires demonstrating that God has a plan and a vision for history. Through Jesus, God is actively engaged in history to bring about the transformation of the present world. Rather than repeating the past, a completely new age has broken in through Jesus. The purpose of history has been fulfilled in Christ and the cycle of the ages has been broken with the advent of God's emerging Kingdom.

Understanding how a variety of myths play out in a given cultural context helps us to customize our articulation of the Gospel to that specific cultural community. It is important to recognize the ways that our own culture interacts with these myths and to interpret the ways that they are at work in our neighbors' culture. This way, we can allow the Gospel to freely challenge each culture as we together encounter God's Kingdom breaking into our world and challenging each of our assumptions.

Chapter 15

Becoming a Spiritual Person

If we want to be trusted when entering into culture, we must understand what the qualities of a trustworthy person are in our new cultural context. If we wish to be seen as spiritual people, we must understand what a spiritual person looks like in the culture we wish to reach. In some West African cultures, a spiritual teacher grows a beard. In previous decades, it was difficult to secure a job as a preacher in some American churches if the minister showed up to the interview wearing a beard, no matter how neatly groomed; professionals in that context were expected to be clean-shaven. However, in West African Muslim contexts, any man who is able, regardless of how fashionably he can sport it, should consider growing a beard if he wishes to be viewed as a teacher of spiritual truths. Growing a beard is not at odds with the Gospel; it does not detract from the message of Jesus. It does, however, help one to be seen as a religious person in at least some cultural settings and thus, can aide in the transmission of the Gospel. Anyone working among the African diaspora might also consider committing parables to memory and practicing their storytelling abilities. Both storytelling and parables are vehicles for conveying truth common among the African cultures we have worked with and contribute to the messenger being seen as a spiritual person.

Contrast this with Bengali culture. One day my friend Rini told me he had to shave his beard before going back to Dhaka to see his mother. "I thought that faithful Muslim men grew beards," I said, "I see many men leaving the Masjid who have beards." "Yes," he answered, "but those are old men. For me it is no good, my mother will pull it out of my face if she sees me. Young men should not have beards." Among my Bengali friends in the city it would not raise my status as a spiritual person if I grew a beard, at least not until I am old. It does matter to them, however, that I wear long pants. They, like many other cultural communities, only allow children to wear shorts. Anyone who wishes to be seen as an adult wears long trousers. In Bengali neighborhoods I also am careful about entering restaurants that are not Muslim-owned. If they serve alcohol or pork, it may be best to avoid eating them in sight of my Muslim friends. In their eyes, a spiritual person does not eat pork or drink alcohol. Even nominal believers who do these things themselves will discredit you as a spiritual person if you do. Although they realize they fall short of their own religious standards, they will initially judge you by that same standard.

My friend Rob grew up in the poorest parts of the Bronx and has a deep disillusionment with the church. One night as we spoke about faith over dinner Rob said, "I don't want to talk about anything important with someone who won't drink with me. If they can't sit down and have a drink with me then they don't have anything to say that I want to hear." This attitude is common among my friends who were raised in the Bronx. I can name a dozen or more contacts—several of whom have joined one of our churches or become Christians—who have said that they like to talk about spiritual things with us because they don't see us as "religious." In this post-Christian community, being attached to the traditional church ethos may make you religious, but it may also make you into someone who is to be avoided by spiritual seekers, as they tend to view religion and spirituality as distinct and potentially mutually exclusive traits.

It is easy to violate customs inadvertently and damage one's reputation in the community. For example, while giving a gift may be a sign of affection or friendship in your culture of origin, it could communicate in your diaspora neighbor's culture that you feel a sense of patronage or status over the recipient. At other times, it may not, and giving a gift could advance the relationship in meaningful ways. Sometimes carrying a Bible that is well worn, highlighted, and annotated may indicate to other American Christians that you treasure your Bible and study it with care, to your Muslim friend it shows that you have no respect for God's word as sacred. It is often good to own an unmarked and well-preserved Bible to carry when studying with Muslims, as the Scriptures are a sacred object that must never be damaged or defaced.

When seeking to be seen as a spiritual person, it is critical to reflect on the myths of inclusion, law, and spiritual power as they are manifested in our neighbor's culture. In an inclusive culture, admonishment or correction might take place in the form of a story to allow the hearer to understand the message inductively without feeling shamed through open rebuke. In a culture that prioritizes myths of spiritual power, it would be nearly impossible to be trusted as a spiritual person if one denies the veracity of those same powers. Each minister must determine personally how much they must empty themselves of their own notion of what is required of a spiritual person and the extent to which they are willing to adapt in order to be seen as a credible witness of the Gospel.

Of course, we recognize that there are examples of Jesus or his followers intentionally behaving in a way that was counter-cultural. Counter-cultural behaviors are certainly a part of our Christian witness. However, it is also important to keep in mind that Jesus and his followers knew their cultural setting intimately. It is helpful remove as many cultural barriers as possible that might stand between our diaspora friend and the Gospel of Christ. Otherwise, what we think as counter-cultural might simply be understood as intentionally offensive. For counter-cultural behaviors to make a statement that points to Jesus, they must take place within the cultural world of the hearer or observer. Only then can any potential counter-cultural behaviors be understood in a way that represents the Good News of God's Kingdom. We suggest that our as our diapora friends become students of the Gospel, they are going to understand how to make counter-cultural statements that accurately represent the Gospel witness to their culture much better than we will as cross-cultural messengers.

As one may observe through these examples, our approach and expectations will need to adjust to the particular cultural community we are encountering. This highlights the importance of becoming attentive observers of culture and of learning to ask good questions. Even as we enter deeply into relationship with members of another culture, we should never stop being learners. Good preparation ought to involve some background research about the culture; if we discover some aspects to be different than expected within the context of a diaspora community, we can adjust our practices. However, basing our starting assumptions on what we know of the country of origin is not a

Mosaic

bad place to begin. From there, we can allow ourselves to be corrected and adapt when working in diaspora communities. Perhaps our diaspora neighbors have had to make adjustments since leaving their country of origin, but we should not expect that they reflect our cultural norms or ways of thinking. Just as they are working hard to adapt to the host culture of their new country, we, as ambassadors of the Gospel, should be prepared to work hard to adapt to the cultural world of their community as well. It is important that we do not become paralyzed by a fear of making mistakes; however, it is equally crucial that we seek to learn all we can about the cultural world of our diaspora neighbors.

We encourage you to take the leap and be willing to make mistakes. At the same time, learn as much as you can. Crossing cultures as messengers of the Gospel is an exciting adventure. We often make mistakes, but crossing cultures for the sake of God's Kingdom, forces us to become better listeners. We regularly have to reflect on our actions or attitudes and ask if we are representing good news to those who might see the world through a different lens. This forces us to constantly come back to the picture of Jesus and ask the hard questions. Crossing cultures as Christ's ambassadors is often hard work, but it is worth every step.

Practice One

Ethnographic Study

Name the three most respected spiritual people in the community you are working in. As you determine who these people might be, think through the following questions:

1. When someone needs advice or counsel, where do they go?

2. How do this culture's myths of inclusion, law, or spiritual power affect who is seen as a spiritual person?

3. What are the issues that might cause a person to seek out spiritual counsel?

4. If people were to judge themselves as not adequately spiritual, what actions would they say are lacking in their daily life?

Notes:

Chapter 16

Sowing the Right Seed

A favorite parable that speaks to our work the parable of the sower (Matt. 13:1-23). The reader will recall that the sower scatters seed on four types of soil: on a path, on rocky soil, on soil choked with thorns, and on good soil. It can relieve a great deal of guilt or emotional pressure to learn that there are some soils that just will not support life and we are free to seek out healthy and receptive ground for cultivation. However, there are times when we may be too quick to dismiss soil as too rocky or too thorny when, in reality, it is perfectly fine soil for the Gospel once it is freed from our cultural trappings. Having worked for a few years in plant nurseries before going into ministry, I (Seth) can attest that where you plant certain things matters a great deal. It may be that the front of your house would be a nice looking place for those impatiens, but the direct sunlight is going to kill them every time. And the poor lucky bamboo you have in the pot on the back porch is going to rot because the soil is not rocky enough to provide good drainage. So in the spirit of sowing good seed on appropriate soil, we would like to suggest a few of the initial evangelistic conversations we like to have in different communities and provide some insight into why we feel that sowing with these seeds is helpful. Numerous approaches to evangelism may be effective under the right circumstances, while others should be discarded. We certainly do not prescribe a one-size-fits-all philosophy as we address the mosaic of cultures embodied in our cities but do hope the approaches we suggest will expand your gardening tool kit as you sow the seeds of the Gospel.

Recognizing Orality

Several years ago I (Jared) was facilitating a small house church in the home of a Dominican friend in New York City. For several months, I had worked with this church to explore faith in God through examination of the Scriptures. We had developed great relationships but the meeting had not grown beyond a small group gathered in that living room. One day when meeting with the host I decided to try a different approach. We turned to one of the Gospels and shared a story together. I then had him repeat the story back to me and asked him to try sharing it with a friend during the week. I came back a week later. He perfectly repeated the story back to me, and then he described how he had shared it with a Jewish friend in the community. Shortly afterwards, he traveled to the Dominican Republic to take care of family matters and was gone several months. When I stopped by to visit after his return nearly a year later, he began telling me the story with near perfect recall. I realized that I had begun ministry with this household without thinking about how reliant I was on written texts as my default mode of teaching. My friend, on the other hand, came from a culture in which knowledge and stories are preserved and passed on as oral texts. Rather than this being an obstacle to my friend engaging the Scriptures, it placed him more comfortably in the tradition of how Scripture has traditionally been learned and transmitted throughout the history of the church—by hearing, telling and repeating stories.

Those of us in Western cultural settings have largely used mission strategies for reaching non-believers that are rooted in the cultural assumptions of a highly literate and logic-based environment. However, many of the world's cultures utilize oral approaches to learning and passing on important matters to the next generation (Casey, 2013, pp. 107–114). In recent years, mission organizations have had a growing awareness that the majority of the world's cultures represent those who are oral learners or—even if they are literate— prefer oral learning. For instance, among many others the International Mission Board began emphasizing oral approaches to evangelism, and International Orality Network has served as a resource for engaging oral or post-literate cultures. A variety of story-telling approaches have been employed to communicate the Gospel, and some mission agencies are training cross-cultural evangelists to become oral story-tellers. "What makes this training effective is the focus on learning a little, practicing a lot, implementing immediately, and telling stories often" (Wiles, July 2015, pp. 333–334).

Our team emphasizes the need for mouth-to-ear evangelism because we want to be a catalyst to help the seeds of the Gospel spread spontaneously from life to life. Anytime we share a story or principle from God's word, we want our hearer to be able to repeat it an hour later. In cultures that pass on ideas primarily through oral communication, we must recognize the need for relational approaches to ministry, as communication takes place through person-to-person interactions (Casey, 2013, p. 114). If we want to see the seeds of the Gospel continue to spread beyond the first hearer, we must communicate in ways that they will find natural to replicate.

Even though many of our contacts prefer oral methods, we do work in North American cities where the majority of the population is literate. Thus, our team usually works towards helping groups of believers engage the text of the Bible to become spiritual "self-feeders." However, we share numerous stories, testimonies, and parables before diving into the text of Scripture. As cross-cultural evangelists engage diaspora communities, it is helpful to commit to memory stories that we believe may communicate good news as a bridge to the cultural groups we are encountering. Remembering Jesus's approach and the nature of oral cultures around the world, cross-cultural ministers shouldn't feel pressured to rush beyond oral sharing if that is indeed connecting with the hearts of their new diaspora friends. Verbally sharing stories can sometimes be the most effective way to plant the seeds of the Gospel and see those seeds replicated beyond the first household.

Honor Evangelism

Many of my (Seth) first spiritual conversations with Muslims begin like this: "After speaking to you, it appears that you are a truly spiritual person. *Isa* (Jesus) told us in the *Injil* (Gospel) that only the person with the right ears would hear the true teaching of *Allah (God)*. Spiritual people like you have the sort of ears he was talking about. I think I would learn many new things if you would teach me about the *Injil*. Would it be alright if I shared some of *Isa's* teaching with you and maybe you could explain to me what it means? " I then proceed to tell parables to my Muslim friend; I have yet to be told "no" when I ask if I can share. My Muslim friends closely value the myth of inclusion, and praise is highly sought after. By accepting the role of teacher, they have raised their status in my eyes and they are generally eager to hear what I might share with them, so that they can demonstrate their understanding of spiritual matters. Coincidentally, by taking the passive position and allowing them to be the interpreter and authority of the parables, I allow the teaching to function much the same way it seems to in Jesus's ministry. That is, it is a litmus test of spiritual understanding as well as a vehicle for teaching about the kingdom.

This practice of taking the lower position and honoring someone as a potential interpreter of the Gospel has proved much more effective than the alternative of setting myself (a cultural outsider to the community) up as an authority of spiritual matters with my Muslim neighbor. And if their interpretation of the parable seems off track from the Gospel, I can respond as I learned from a non-Western friend, "What you say is very good, but let me add something." Then I can tell another story or parable that pushes against the misguided interpretation I received before.

Taking this sort of approach feels counter-intuitive and may feel a bit risky. However, it opens the door for the word of God to enter a discussion, and it draws in the non-believer to begin participating in the interpretation of the Bible, not unlike a discussion-based Bible study. By placing the primacy on the Scriptures rather than our role as the teacher, it calls on us, as the evangelists, to trust the transformational power of the Word. This strategy for starting discussions about Scripture is sensitive to those originating from cultures that prioritize the myth of inclusion, and by taking note of their cultural concern for shame and honor, we have lowered potential defenses that typically rise in inter-religious discussions. Conversion stories from overseas missionaries in Muslim contexts often describe a fairly drawn out relational process. By taking a humble position and honoring our Muslim neighbors, we are able to stay engaged rather than potentially finding ourselves cut off because of perceived threatening conversations. It also helps the evangelist identify those who are potentially receptive to the Gospel by listening to their interpretations of stories from Scripture. This approach to sowing opens a pathway for engaging the Gospel in a way that is non-threatening to our Muslim friends.

Beatitude Evangelism

Similarly, with many of my post-Christian friends, I (Seth) begin by identifying in them one of the blessings with which Jesus began the Sermon on the Mount. I might say, "You are a real peacemaker" or "You are always comforting mourning people," or even "You refuse to use your position to run over other people, I think your meekness is a lot like Jesus." I explicitly tell my friend that this quality is like Jesus. Most post-Christians are not used to religious people comparing them favorably to Jesus; it is generally quite the opposite, so you might imagine how this approach stirs their attention! Then I ask my friend to use this quality to help me in a difficult situation. As I minister, I usually have some point of conflict easily at hand from one of our various church groups or leadership teams. I present the issue in a general way without revealing any specific identities to my non-religious friend and then say, "You are already like Jesus in this way, how would you advise me to act as a Christian?" It is rare that anyone turns down the chance to help me out. By taking the lower place and letting them compare and contrast themselves with Jesus, much of the evangelistic work is done for me. And if their advice seems off track from the values of the Gospel, all I have to say is, "I could see why you would say that, but that goes against this other value of Jesus that I also have to maintain in the situation. What other suggestions can you think of?"

This approach identifies a bridge for the Gospel by identifying a positive quality already present in the person's character. For individuals who have experienced rejection and ridicule by religious people, beginning a dialog with affirmation may open the door for engagement with the Gospel. It also subtly places the authority of Scripture at the center of the conversation. The evangelist places herself in a position of vulnerability and draws the non-believer into figuring out how to best apply the teachings of Jesus. By asking them to help us act more like Jesus, we are not only testifying to the humility of Christ among our neighbors but are drawing our post-Christian friend into deeper engagement with the teachings of the Gospel.

Contrasting (Bad) Examples with Christ

Christian ministers often mourn the bad examples of ministry or overly pushy styles of evangelism, but what if we decided to turn these moments on their head and use them to point to Christ? New York is always a hub of street-preaching and proselytism. Whether it is the Jehovah's Witnesses, headquartered in Brooklyn, the store-front church on the corner, or the Alex Jones doomsday conspiracy theorist, it is never hard to find someone on the street shouting into a microphone or passing out religious tracts. Rather than simply roll my eyes and walk on, this can be a good opportunity to open up a conversation with a stranger about the Gospel. "I hate this stuff man," I will say to my neighbor on the train, as the subway preacher begins literally to damn those on the subway bench across from us. "I understand what he is after, but it does not look like what I see in Jesus." If my neighbor is interested, now I have a point of contrast. Odds are, my new friend has seen this type of evangelism day in and day out for years. But he may have never had any Christian just gently and civilly start a conversation about Jesus without a dogmatic agenda. In our urban setting, complaining about religion-gone-bad is often a great way to start a conversation about what Christianity is really about. Rather than feel defensive ourselves about bad practices on display, we may instead attempt to refocus on the nature of Christ. Sometimes poor evangelism practices or even bad examples of Christianity in general may become a prop for refocusing on the good news of Jesus.

Conclusion

As we reach out, start relationships, and communicate good news beyond cultural boundaries, it will be important to reflect on whether the approaches most natural to us might seem completely foreign to our neighbors from around the world. These examples shared above are only a few approaches that might feel new to many of us. We wanted to share them precisely because of their counter-intuitive nature. However, this is not at all meant to be exhaustive or definitive in any way.

In addition, as we seek to demonstrate the love of Christ to multiethnic communities and encounter those we might describe as "post-Christian" or perhaps post-religious in general, we should be cautious about utilizing evangelism or church growth methods that they have already encountered and previously rejected. Sometimes "old" methods may be effective because they are old enough to be "new" again or have never been experienced in different cultural context. Sometimes methods that fail to make an impact an impact in one culture can make a big difference in another one, or sometimes something that might be worn out in a diaspora community's culture of origin might connect as nostalgic when reaching the diaspora. The point is, we should evaluate what will build a bridge to a particular cultural community rather than assume we just apply our standard methods from within our own culture. By recognizing factors such as the role of oral cultures, the dynamics of honor & shame, or the various myths that are in conflict playing out around us, we can grow in our impact as messengers of good news of God's Kingdom.

Chapter 17

Getting Your Church Started

Some who read this will have the resources at hand in their churches to incorporate diaspora ministry into an existing program. Others may already have an idea of how reaching out to their diaspora neighbors fits into their existing vision and ministry. For everyone else, however, we want to give a few possible guidelines for beginning work with your diaspora neighbors. The following will be listed in terms of steps, but are not necessarily chronological. Several of the steps will be happening simultaneously, and the pace will be different depending on a number of factors: openness of the community, training needs of church members, etc.

The first step is to identify who your neighbors are. Find the major businesses owned by immigrant peoples in your area, visit them, learn what countries and regions the community immigrated from and how long they have been in the US, find a book about the history of that region or people group, etc. It is likely that when you look around, there will be more than one major diaspora community in your area. Some diaspora communities will be centrally located because they have clustered together and begun to form an ethnic enclave. Others may be scattered across the city but are often linked together as an ethnic network. They may have common places where they relationally connect like tea rooms, ethnic markets, restaurants, or associations.

The second step, is to begin prayerfully assessing where you and your church want to reach out. Maybe you have Iraqi Christians down the block who have fled to the US because of political instability and persecution in their homeland; this would be a very different ministry than reaching out to West African Muslims or to Central American migrants. It is important that you and your ministry team come to a prayerful discernment of who you are reaching out to and to what end. Few churches are able to effectively focus on more than one major culture or sustain multiple streams of cross-cultural ministry. Learning a culture well and forming cross-cultural relationships are difficult tasks. It is a rare church that can simultaneously plant a church, sustain a refugee ministry, host an ethnic congregation in their building, and offer an ESL program all while keeping the standards of excellence high in all the ministries offered. We would recommend specializing where you feel that God has best equipped your church and focusing on doing that ministry to the best of your ability. Once a ministry is established and self-sustaining, you can always look at adding other facets of cross-cultural engagement.

The third step is to begin casting vision. If you are the preacher or on the worship planning team, this is a good time to go back to Scripture and see the concern that the Bible has for the immigrant and the foreigner. It seems that many Christians do not realize just how strongly the Bible teaches us to love foreigners or immigrants and how favorably it sees the exile or refugee. Learning to love the immigrant as we love ourselves is an act of obedience of God's word. If you want to begin shaping the vision of your church, it most often starts in the pulpit, the worship, and the conversation that happens in your Bible classes or small groups. The goal is to give the congregation the lens and the theological language you want them reading the text through. You want to be training them to look beyond their cultural assumptions and to be naturally asking the question: What does this passage say about the immigrant? How do we obey God's call to reach the nations right here in our midst? Vision-casting is meant to reorient the church's perception of the word immigrant from something that belongs to the sphere of the evening news or political debates to something that is essential to any conversation about the Gospel. How do we love all of our neighbors? The best way to do that is to use the language Scripture gives us; reclaim the vocabulary used everyday so that when your church hears it, the connotation is now one of mission. When church members hear the term "immigrant," rather thinking in political terms do they begin thinking about missions opportunities in their backyard? When the answer to this is yes, then you have successfully begun to cast a vision for loving your diaspora neighbor. We have attached some suggestions on this subject in the appendices at the end of this work.

The fourth step, and one of the most important, is to identify your leaders. Cross-cultural ministry requires a lot of time and relational investment. Chances are that not everyone will be able to commit time and effort to this ministry. While you do want the whole church praying and supporting the work, you will need a team that is prepared to invest as learners. It is important that you have a group of people who will be consistent, who are flexible learners, and who are willing to sow a lot of seeds without becoming discouraged by slow-growing fruit. Your church may encounter a highly receptive community, or it may attempt to reach a group that is strongly resistant to the message of the Gospel and its messengers. The cross-cultural team should be prepared for a range of scenarios.

There are many ways you can go about finding the right team: you can start a Bible class or new small group devoted to starting this ministry, you can hand-pick a team based on mission experience, you can hire a full-time person to head up the ministry. It is important to remember, though, that smaller is almost always better in this kind of work. Sending a team of 10 or 12 outsiders into a small, culturally different neighborhood will easily overwhelm most diaspora communities and serve to highlight the cultural distance that already exists, which makes it harder to conduct the kind of research needed for really deep and attentive learning about the culture. A team of 10 or 12 would often need to split into pairs when out in the community and seeking to start evangelistic conversations. A large group of outsiders coming into an ethnic neighborhood can be overwhelming. Our rule of thumb would be not to have more people on your team than can easily (and somewhat inconspicuously) go out to eat together at the most popular restaurant in your target community. A larger team will often need to be divided into smaller sub-teams with each smaller unit focusing on a different area or set of relationships. Again, the most important qualities you can find in your leaders are consistency, flexibility, and a learning attitude.

Once you have a team and a particular people group identified, the next step is to become regulars. Begin frequenting popular businesses owned and operated by the community, learn names, learn a few words (at the very least "hello," "thank you," "good bye") in their heart language—essentially become "known" people in the community and begin forming initial relationships. This is something you as the minister leading the new work can begin today, before any other steps are taken. It is difficult to overestimate how far being a kind and well-tipping patron of an immigrant-owned business can go towards opening the doors for relationships. Once you feel that you are remembered and recognized in the neighborhood, begin bringing your potential team members out to the restaurant or the deli with you. This is where they can initiate early participant observation and begin developing ethnographic skills.

If you are in a large city with many different cultural groups spread across a metro area, you may want to begin forming an alliance for local missions. It would be easy for every church to want to send a team of people to the one Iraqi neighborhood of a few hundred people. However, if several churches in the city are coming together and forging a collaboration, a strategic vision for bringing good news across the cultural mosaic of the city may begin to emerge. That doesn't mean that different ministries can't work in the same community, but being in collaborative conversations can help avoid territorial disputes between ministries or accidentally undermining one another's efforts. This sort of communication also helps to highlight areas of need where no ministries are currently engaged. For instance, there may be several ministries reaching out—both separately and together—to Spanish-speaking communities and to Muslim groups, but as ministry leaders begin to communicate with each other, they begin to discover that no one is attempting to reach a growing Buddhist community from Southeast Asia or a well-established Russian Jewish population. With this need identified through communication and collaboration, a church or ministry leader may answer the call to fill that gap in their cities evangelistic initiatives. Such communication across diaspora ministries in a metro area together sharing a Kingdom vision for the city can identify gaps or areas of need that would otherwise be overlooked. The larger the city, the more unlikely it will be that you know every ministry well enough to bring everyone together, but developing such collaborations to the highest degree possible will go a long way to facilitating Kingdom growth in the city. As leaders come together and dialog with one another, they are able to share resources and discuss what they are learning with each other. Each person's cultural learning increases since no one is experiencing these lessons in a vacuum. Forming collaborative conversations across various diaspora ministries in an area is a way of moving beyond our local ministries and embracing a broader Kingdom vision for the city.

Conclusion

Culture has always been important. Furthermore, North America has always been a mission field. However, today these consistent realities are more obvious than ever. In contemporary mission efforts, many church planters and leaders have embraced the opportunity to move beyond the colonial past to see the Gospel become fully embodied in the culture that hosts them. They apply a set of principles and practices that generates a growing understanding of the culture around them, so they are able to cross cultural bridges in order to help new believers contextualize the Gospel among their own community. In our global era, missionary perspectives and practices have become quite practical for local ministry as we go next door and across town. The ends of the earth are within reasonable reach of the average member of an American church.

There are two important cautions that we want to emphasize again at the conclusion of this book. They might seem contradictory but are actually quite compatible as related points of concern for local mission leaders going forward. First, we want to caution yet one more time about assuming our own cultural perspectives and behaviors are somehow synonymous with the Gospel itself. At this point in the book, if you are reading the conclusion, we are making the bold assumption that we are all the same page on that basic point. However, it is worth repeating, and we want to offer an accompanying point of caution as well.

Secondly, we want to warn our readers to avoid becoming paralyzed due to a fear of making mistakes or continually feeling like we don't know enough. That, of course, is the risk of producing a book such as this one. It is easy to fall into the trap of inaction because we feel that we never quite know enough to begin, and as a result, the first step is always delayed. This easily leads to paralysis. The reality is we will make mistakes. We will sometimes be misunderstood, and we will misunderstand others. We will never be fully inside of the culture even as we are fully accepted by our diaspora neighbors to participate within it. This shouldn't be a cause for discouragement; rather this admission of our natural limitations ought to be empowering because we are learning on-the-job. When we recognize that imperfection is the norm, we can proceed with boldness. We need to be willing to take risks and to take the first step. The world is changing so quickly that inaction is just not an option.

While we hope that the tools and applications found in this book will help to increase the effectiveness of cross-cultural ministers in what has become a global society, there is one underlying theme that we wish every reader to internalize: to be learners. Crossing cultures requires us to become students of those we are reaching, and as a consequence, we also never stop learning about ourselves. One of the surprising and wonderful aspects of cross-cultural mission is that we too are transformed.

As ambassadors of the Gospel of reconciliation, we have unprecedented opportunities to embrace our calling as a missionary people among the nations living next door. Building on the foundations of missionary practices, today's church faces a world unimagined by previous generations of mission leaders. The city has become a sea of cultures; we pray you will take the plunge.

Appendix 1

Questions for Contextualization

These questions represent a "cheat sheet" some of our teams use when doing ethnographic work. They help us to investigate the myths we think most likely to present bridges and barriers to the Gospel when beginning to learn about our neighbor's culture. Having the various issues brought together as a list helps us to quickly revisit what issues we lack understanding in and to quickly compare notes with other teammates about what we're learning.

The 3 levels of worldview
- How does the Gospel serve as/speak to
    o knowledge/beliefs
    o feelings/behaviors
    o allegiance/values

Worldview (WV) provides
- cognitive foundations
- emotional support
- validates deep cultural norms
- integrates new experiences into culture
- monitors cultural change

Initial Questions

- How institutionalized is caste/class?
  - Can one change classes?
  - Does the diaspora effect status change?
  - What professions correspond to what class?
- What are the economic median and poles?
- What are forms of currency?
  - Social, material, religious, etc.
- What is the gender vs. age strata?
  - Rank the following in terms of status (who can have authority over whom)
    - Children
    - Young Men
    - Young Women
    - Fathers
    - Mothers
    - Grandparents
    - Unrelated Elders
- How is age perceived?
- What technologies are considered original to this culture?
- How ceremonial is everyday life?
- What words in the vernacular have both religious and nonreligious functions/meanings?
- What is the major industry in the local economy?
- What is the history with colonialism?
- Name the most observed security needs?
  - Financial

- o   Religious fidelity
- o   Cohesion of the family
- o   Retaining of cultural identity
- o   Difficulty of assimilating
- o   Etc.
- What are present threats to the life of the community?
- Develop a hierarchy of scheduling importance
    - o   work, family, communal events, religious observance, sleep, recreation, gender specific activities, etc.
- Who are historical enemies?
    - o   Who are victims and who the oppressors?

Questions of time

- Is a linear or apocalyptic view of time necessary in order to identify with the Gospel?
    - o   Linear perspective ask, "How did it begin, how will it end?"
- How to engage cyclical time?
    - o   In American culture, what is a healthy temporal aspect of post-progressivism?
- Further issues of time to consider-
    - o   Genealogical function of history
        - ▪   the holding up of past individuals who represent, and so ensure, the values of the present
        - ▪   historical narratives which transform the mundanity of present actions/community into something heroic and legitimate
    - o   Memorialization function of history

- Annals of day to day which heighten importance of tradition and transform seemingly insignificant actions of daily life into statements of value through recollection and observation

- Other temporal constructs
  - 3 part-
    - Mythical Past
    - Recent (Ancestral) Past
    - Present (with incorporation of near future)
  - Situationally oriented
    - adoptive narratives of past as "case-study" for present
    - little identification with historical past

Questions of Authority/Power

- Issues of discipline
  - How and what do they punish?
  - Who has the ability to extend mercy/determine sufficiency?
  - What are the mechanisms of chastisement?
  - Is there delay between the mechanics of punishment and social re-embrace?
  - Who do appeals go to after initial judgment?
  - How public must censorship be to establish recompense?
  - What is the subjugated knowledge operating within established narratives

- Identify minority subcultures under presenting culture
- Name battles for definitive powers within the spectrum of assimilation
  - where do these battles take place and between what subgroups/sub-narratives?
  - is the field of conflict characterized by a schismatic or domineering agenda

What form does civil disobedience take?

Is legality or tradition appealed to more frequently to establish a violation?

What is relationship to sovereign state or body of laws/traditions?

Who has the power to adopt or approve new laws/traditions?

Outside of formal punishment, what are the mechanisms of social coercion?

- Issues of patronage, knowledge and care
  o What is the role of gift-giving in establishing relationships of power?
  o Is hosting a part of or an impediment to moral authority (review for both cultural insider and outsider)?
  o What is the link between patronage and teaching?
  o Is wisdom or insight an expected element of pastoral care?
  o How else is solidarity expressed?
  o How does one become a trusted person?

- What are the characteristics of one who is trusted in this culture?
- How does one lose trust?
- Regain? Can trust be regained?
- How does humor function?
  - Who can tease who?
  - Who can voice offense and who cannot?
- How does one assimilate into a group?
- How do groups express cohesion?
  - Nicknames
  - Slang
  - Special Clothing
- How does one amicably leave a group?
- What are the expectations of displaced/non-proximal members?
- What is the authority distance between leaders/bosses and others?
- What is the level of formality in relationships of disparate authority?
- Equal authority?
- How is authority established?
- Does knowledge reside in the individual, the community, or a codified tradition?
- Of what social value is wisdom?
- What is the role of specialization vs generalization in education/training?
- What are the expectations of education?

- o What is the level of lay engagement in institutions of science/knowledge?
- o Is moral knowledge seen as separate from other bodies of knowledge?

- Issues of ceremony and its functions
  - o What is the liturgical life of the community?
    - Weddings, Funerals, rituals of birth, rituals of puberty, coronations, elections, national holidays, religious festivals,etc
  - o What is the contextual origin of each celebration?
    - Appeals to agriculture or husbandry
    - Appeals to historical figures and events
    - Appeals to religious myths
  - o Do these ceremonies primarily function as a demonstration of present society's continuity with mythic value or to intensify power through spectacle/fascination? (Thanksgiving vs. Independence day)
  - o What, if any, are the metaphysical aims of each ceremony?
  - o What is the role of state in ceremony?
  - o What ceremonial adoption has taken place in diaspora?
  - o What technologies have been grafted into or denied access into ceremony? (e.g. Spring Festival in China and Television)

Questions of myth and structure

- What is the architecture/geography of the community?
  - What areas make up the center of community life? What's "downtown?"
- Who are the mythic/historical heroes?
  - Of majority
  - Of minority
  - Of adults only
  - Of children only
- Who are the present heroes (meaning within the last two generations)?
- Who wears a uniform and what does it represent?
- Who are the mythical characters for which institutionalized roles serve as placeholders?
  - The judge, the law officer, the head of state, the head of family, etc.
- What are points of conflict between traditional myth and new in the diaspora?
  - e.g. the role of business owners vs. religious elders in Bronx Bengali community
- How does denial function in these conflicts?
- How is cognitive dissonance (CD) resolved?
  - Proselytism, Effort Justification, etc.
- How is it expressed?
  - What is the degree of awareness of CD?
- What myths involved in CD go unrecognized by the community?

- What myths have passed through CD to be contextualized and integrated into the community?
- How have rituals retained outward structure but transferred allegiance to new narratives?

-What words or phrases express the identity of the culture?

Appendix 2

Preaching Care for the Immigrant from Scripture

The following is an excerpt from one of our team blogs. We feel that it is a good example of a teaching which begins to reclaim the language of immigration from Scripture to begin casting vision for cross-cultural ministry.

"We're working with immigrants." I cringe almost every time I have to say it so bluntly. I am now in the Bronx, working with diaspora people groups in the Five Boroughs of New York City. And yes, we're primarily working with immigrants; and it is such a large work to be done: The total global diaspora numbers in the millions and includes hundreds of distinct people groups. A larger number of those peoples settle in the U.S. than in any other host country, making a large portion of the United States foreign born. It's an incredible chance to share the message of Jesus and to form cross-cultural relationships which more genuinely reflect something deeply important about the Kingdom of God. In major cities like New York, but also in unexpected places like my (Seth's) hometown of Amarillo, there exist significant pockets of immigrant people groups who we can no longer think of as "those others over there." They're our neighbors, and Jesus says we're supposed to love our neighbors.

But they're also immigrants, and that term carries an embarrassing weight in our culture. It seems like in celebrating our

263

great opportunity to share the Gospel, I've planted myself in the middle of a political debate. Where I come from, calling someone an immigrant implies an abhorrent "otherness;" our media is not kind in its portrayal of those from around the world who seek asylum behind its walls. We are surrounded by narratives of nationalism that seek to make us afraid of those who don't look like us and don't come from where we do. And let me be the first to confess: My Gospel at times has been co-opted. But let me also confess that I want to redeem my sinful and stingy imagination. Let us see if we can't remember an alternative narrative, and if we might not reclaim the deep resonances and reverence Scripture caries for the immigrant.

It starts with Abraham. God chose a family and made them migrants. They didn't know where they were immigrating to, but they remained vagrant into the fourth generation before settling in Egypt. God's immigrants stayed there for 400 years, but always as a second class people. They remained aliens and foreigners even in this land. And God brought them out of Egypt with a mighty hand and they became migrants in the desert for two generations.

Their understanding of transience is reflected in the law God gives them: "You shall not oppress the alien, for you know the heart of an alien" (Ex. 23:9); "The alien who resides among you shall be to you as the citizen among you; you shall love the alien as yourself, for you were aliens" (Lv. 19:34); "The Lord your God is God of gods...who executes justice for the orphan and the widow, and who loves the foreigner...You shall also love the foreigner for you were foreigners" (Duet. 10:19). And Israel's failure to follow this specific command is listed highly in the prophets among the reasons for their exile, "I will draw near to you for judgment, I will be swift to bear witness against the sorcerers, against the adulterers...against those who oppress the hired workers in their wages, the widow and the orphan, against those who thrust aside the alien and do not fear me" (Mal. 3:5).

The great-grandmother of Israel's greatest king was an immigrant, and Matthew lists four immigrant women in the genealogy of Jesus. Because it is among a diaspora minority that the Messiah was born and he, himself, became an African refugee to Egypt before he was even old enough to know the land of his birth. The same Messiah sent his disciples among all the nations of the world as migrant minorities; and it was through a network of immigrants like Paul, Priscilla and Aquila, and Apollos that the church spread through the dominant empire.

The story of Scripture and the narrative of God's people is an immigrant's tale. God's people are always called to be strangers, aliens, foreigners in a spiritual sense, but they're also called to look out for and care for those who are literal migrants in their midst as they themselves are often migrants.

So it seems that perhaps we in the Western church have been guilty of letting our culture speak where Scripture has already spoken. It seems that we have exchanged the narrative of a God who is creating one people from every tongue and tribe, to a God who favors our tribe: a Gospel that sounds like the story the rest of the world tells. It seems that as the nations of the world come to us, we must be challenged to remember that God has called us to be a blessing to and to make disciples of all nations.

Bibliography

The Bangladeshi Diaspora in the United States (July 2014).
http://www.migrationpolicy.org/research/select-diaspora-
populations-united-states: The Migration Policy Institute

Barker, C. (2003). *Cultural Studies: Theory and Practice* (2nd ed.). London,
U.K.: Sage Publications.

Beard, M. (2015). *SPQR: A History of Ancient Rome*. New York, NY: Liveright
Publishing Corporation.

Bernard, H. R. (2006). *Research Methods in Anthropology: Qualitative and
Quantitative Approaches* (Fourth Edition ed.). Lanham, MD: Alta
Mira Press

Bouchelle, S. (January 28, 2013). Questions I'm Asking. *Summit 2013
Podcast*. Retrieved from
https://itunes.apple.com/us/podcast/questions-i-am-
asking/id808204738?i=242113224&mt=2

Campbell, J. (1991). *The Power of Myth*. New York, NY: Anchor Books.

Casey, A. (2013). The Rise of Orality in Modern Missions Practice In C. Ott &
J. D. Payne (Eds.), *Missionary Methods: Research, Reflections, and
Realities* (Vol. 21, pp. 107–126). Pasadena, CA: William Carey Library

Chamberlain, L. K. (2002). Durgā and the Dashain Harvest Festival: From the
Indus to Kathmandu Valleys. *ReVision, 25*(1), 24–32.

Chernus, I. (2012). The Meaning of "Myth" in the American Context. Retrieved from mythicamerica.wordpress.com/the-meaning-of-myth-in-the-american-context

Clark, C. (2013). *The Sleepwalkers: How Europe Went to War in 1914.* New York: Harper Collins

Cohen, R. (1997). *Global Diasporas: An Introduction.* Seattle, WA: University of Washington Press

De La Torre, M. A. (2004). *Santeria: The Beliefs and Rituals of a Growing Religion in America.* Grand Rapids, MI: Eerdmans.

Deleuze, G., & Guattari, F. (1987). *A Thousand Plateaus: Capitalism and Schizophrenia.* London: Athlone Press Ltd.

Denny, F. M. (1994). *An Introduction to Islam* (Second ed.). New York: MacMillan Publishing Company.

Donovan, V. (1978). *Christianity Rediscovered.* Maryknoll, New York: Orbis Books.

Doty, W. G. (2004). *Myth: A handbook.* Westport, CT: Greenwood Publishing Group.

Esposito, J. L., Fasching, D. J., & Lewis, T. (2007). *Religion and Globalization: World Religions in Historical Perspective.* New York, NY: Oxford University Press.

Ezigbo, V. I., & Williams, R. (2014). Converting a Colonialist Christ: Toward an African Postcolonial Christology. In K. H. Smith, J. Lalitha, & L. D. Hawk (Eds.), *Evangelical Postcolonial Conversations: Global Awakenings in Theology and Praxis*. Downers Grove, IL: Intervarsity Press.

Festinger, L., Riecken, H., & Schachter, S. (2009). *When Prophecy Fails*. London: Pinter & Martin.

Foucault, M. (1978). *The History of Sexuality* (Vol. 1). New York: Random House

Foucault, M. (1997). *Society Must Be Defended: Lectures at the College De France 1975–1976*. New York: Picador.

Geertz, C. (1973). *The Interpretation of Cultures. New York, NY:* Basic Books.

Georges, J. (2014). The 3D Gospel: Ministry in Guilt, Shame, and Fear Cultures. Retrieved from www.HonorShame.com/3DGospel/

Hiebert, P. G. (1987). Critical contextualization. *International Bulletin of Missionary Research, 11*(3), 104-112.

Hiebert, P. G. (2008). *Transforming Worldviews: An Anthropological Understanding of How People Change*. Grand Rapids, MI: Baker Academic.

Hiebert, P. G., Shaw, R. D., & Tienou, T. (2000). *Understanding Folk Religion: A Christian Response to Popular Beliefs and Practices*. Grand Rapids, MI: Baker Books.

Im, C. H., & Casiño, T. C. (2014). Introduction. In C. H. Im & A. Yong (Eds.), *Global Diasporas and Mission*. Portland, OR: Wipf & Stock Publishers

Khlevniuk, O. V. (2015). *Stalin: A New Biography of a Dictator*. New Haven, CT: Yale University Press.

Korda, M. (2010). *Hero: The Life and Legend of Lawrence of Arabia*. New York, NY: HarperCollins.

Kraft, C. H. (2008). *Worldview for Christian witness*. Pasadena, CA: William Carey Library.

Laguerre, M. S. (2003). *Urban Multiculturalism and Globalization in New York City*. New York, NY: Palgrave Macmillan.

Leonard, J. (January 1, 2004). The Church Between Cultures: Rethinking the Church in Light of Global Immigration. Retrieved from http://www.wts.edu/resources/westminsterspeaks/2004/01/01/the_church_between_cultures_rethinking_the_church_in_light_of_globalization_of_immigration.html

Lingenfelter, S. (2003). *Ministering Cross-Culturally: An Incarnational Model of Personal Relationships*. Grand Rapids, MI: Baker Academic

Looney, J. (2015). *Crossroads of the Nations: Diaspora, Globalization, and Evangelism*. Portland, OR: Urban Loft Publishers

Luzbetak, L. J. (2015). *The Church and Cultures: New Perspectives in Missiological Anthropology*. Maryknoll, New York: Orbis Books.

Maich, K. H. (2014). Reducing Cognitive Dissonance Through Effort Justification: Evidence From Past Studies and Daily Experience. *Western Undergraduate Psychology Journal, 1*(1).

Manchester, W., & Reid, P. (2012). *The Last Lion: Winston Spencer Churchill: Defender of the Realm 1940–1965.* New York, NY: Bantam Books.

Marx, K., & Engels, F. (2008). *The Communist Manifesto.* Herfordshire, UK: Wordsworth.

McCurdy, D. W., Spradley, J. P., & Shandy, D. J. (2004). *The Cultural Experience: Ethnography in Complex Society.* Long Grove, IL Waveland Press.

Moschella, M. C. (2008). *Ethnography as Pastoral Practice: An Introduction.* Cleveland, OH: The Pilgrim Press.

Ortiz, M. (1996). *One New People: Models for Developing a Multiethnic Church.* Downers Grove, IL: InterVarsity Press.

Ortiz, M., & Conn, H. M. (2001). *Urban Ministry: The Kingdom, the City & the People of God.* Downers Grove, IL: InterVarsity Press.

Payne, J. D. (2012). *Strangers Next Door: Immigration, Migration, and Mission.* Downers Grove, IL: Intervarsity Press.

Price, M., & Benton-Short, L. (January 1, 2007). Counting Immigrants in Cities Across the Globe *Migration Information Source.* Retrieved from http://www.migrationpolicy.org/article/counting-immigrants-cities-across-globe

Roberts, A. (2014). *Napoleon: A Life*. New York, NY: Penguin Random House

Roembke, L. (2000). *Building Credible Multicultural Teams*. Pasadena, CA: William Carey Library.

Rynkiewich, M. (2012). *Soul, Self, and Society: A Postmodern Anthropology for Mission in a Postcolonial World*. Portland, OR: Wipf and Stock Publishers.

Sagás, E. A Case of Mistaken Identity: Antihaitianismo in Dominican Culture. Retrieved from http://faculty.webster.edu/corbetre/haiti/misctopic/dominican/anti haiti.htm. Date accessed: September 6, 2016.

Scott, A. J., Agnew, J., Soja, E. W., & Storper, M. (2001). Global City–Regions: An Overview.. Oxford: Oxford University Press.

Sheldrake, P. (2007). *A Brief History of Spirituality*. Malden, MA: Blackwell Publishing.

Singer, A., Hardwick, S. W., & Brettell, C. B. (July/August 2008). 21st Century Gateways: Immigrants in Suburban America. *Poverty & Race*.

Spradley, J. (1979). *The Ethnographic Interview*. Belmont, CA: Wadsworth.

Stacey, J. (2009). Unhitching the Horse from Carriage: Love and Marriage Among the Mosuo. *Utah L. Rev.*, 287-321.

Stewart, E., & Bennett, M. (1991). *American Cultural Patterns: A Cross-Cultural Perspective* (Revised ed.): Yarmouth, ME: Intercultural Press, Inc.

Stull, D., & Broadway, M. (2008). Meatpacking and Mexicans on the High Plains: From Minority to Majority in Garden City, Kansas. In R. C. Jones (Ed.), *Immigrants Outside Megalopolis: Ethnic Transformation in the Heartland* (pp. 115–133). Lanham, MD: Lexington Books.

Wan, E., & Casey, A. (2014). *Church Planting among Immigrants in U.S. Urban Centers: The "Where", "Why", And "How" of Diaspora Missiology in Action*. Portland, OR: Institute of Diaspora Studies.

Warner, R. S., & Wittner, J. G. (1998). *Gatherings in Diaspora: Religious Communities and the New Immigration*. Philadelphia, PA: Temple University Press.

Watson, D. & Watson, P. (2014). *Contagious Discipleship Making: Leading Others on a Journey of Discovery*. Nashville, TN: Thomas Nelson.

Wiles, J. (July 2015). A Practitioner/Trainer Perspective on Orality. *Evangelical Missions Quarterly, 51*(3).

Wink, W. (1992). *Engaging the Powers: Discernment and Resistance in a World of Domination*. Minneapolis, MN: Augsburg Fortress.

INDEX

Made in the USA
Lexington, KY
28 March 2017